Canada, what's left?

June 1986

Pat,

Best of luck, Pat.
Could not have written
this without you. I'll
try and be on time
next time.

John

Canada, what's left?

A new social contract pro and con

Edited by
John Richards and
Don Kerr

NeWest Press

First Edition

Canadian Cataloguing in Publication Data

Richards, John and Don Kerr, eds.
Canada: What's Left?

ISBN 0-920316-99-9   (bound)   — ISBN 0-920316-97-2   (pbk.)

1. New Democratic Party – Addresses, essays, lectures.
I. Richards, John.   II. Kerr, Don.
JL197.N4C3 1986   324.27107   C86-091102-0

Credits

Cover and book design: Susan Colberg
Typesetting: Simon Fraser University
Printing and binding: Friesen Printers Limited

Financial Assistance

Alberta Culture
The Canada Council

NeWest Publishers Limited
Suite 204, 8631 - 109 Street
Edmonton, Alberta
Canada T6G 1E8

*to Grant Notley, who practised politics with passion,
with humanity and with humour*

Table of Contents

Acknowledgments

The principal ingredient from which this book was prepared was a transcript of the words and ideas of those who participated in a seminar sponsored by the Department of Political Science at the University of Alberta on the 4th and 5th May, 1984. We have severely edited to avoid repetition and to emphasize the main themes. In so doing we inevitably cut some meat as well as fat. All those whose essays and interventions we have retained receive acknowledgment via brief biographies. However they comprise only half those who were present. We hereby thank all the others.

In addition to the seminar participants, many of whom paid their own way, we thank in particular several people who played a major role in organization of the seminar and in subsequent preparation of this book. Larry Pratt helped with much of the planning, and chaired several sessions. Audrey Bell-Hiller bore the brunt of the administrative responsibility, aided by Lorraine Duncan (at the time Grant Notley's secretary) and Tricia Smith. Fred Engelmann, as chairman of the host department, graciously sponsored several functions for seminar participants. Jack Lewis, manager of Newest Press, calmly and competently organized publication in an impressively short period of time. Ellen Sangster at Simon Fraser University undertook computer typesetting.

The Faculty of Business Administration at Simon Fraser University, the Political Science Department at the University of Alberta and the Alberta New Democratic Party made financial contributions towards the seminar expenses and ultimate publication of the proceedings.

John Richards & Don Kerr
January 1986

Preface

Don Kerr

The essays and debates in this book are based on the proceedings of a two-day seminar held in Edmonton in May, 1984, the origins of which are described by John Richards in his introduction. The seminar proceedings were taped and we have edited the tapes into this form, and added two additional essays to complement the discussion. In great part the editing has meant translating spoken into written prose, without disturbing the essential content or argument. The written accounts are generally more economical and tightly argued than the original speeches, although they have lost in translation something of the individual tone and liveliness of the spoken voice. All participants have read and approved their contributions; some have chosen to make minor improvements to their arguments.

The purpose of the seminar was to debate a new "social contract" between organized labour and government as a central strategy for the federal New Democratic Party to advocate. The two basic principles for a proposed new Canadian social contract were an incomes policy plus an extension of industrial democracy. Remember this was May, 1984 when the federal NDP had lost half its traditional support in the polls and was hovering at 10%, and the 1982 defeat of the Saskatchewan NDP was very much alive for many participants. There was a sense of urgency about redefining the NDP agenda, though little consensus about what policies to follow. So a debate there was, with strong opinions expressed on both sides. In fact because the organizers of the seminar, John Richards and Larry Pratt, were aware of the divergences and wanted the debate to be open, opposition to a new social contract was at least as strong as support for it.

John Richards was interested in using the seminar as a means to advocate a new policy for the NDP. Yet the seminar concluded without any unanimity on the social contract, or any other issue. Given the wide range of participants invited the outcome was probably predictable. Personally I delighted in the process, regardless of any particular outcome. Each speaker of course had a position he tried to convince others to accept, but each position was immediately replaced by another, usually equally well stated. The high point for me came in the discussions where the alternatives replaced each other most rapidly and persuasively. It was first-rate political theatre, a great pleasure in itself. This book may indeed be more valuable for the process it reveals than for the answers it provides. As Allan Blakeney says, "The process whereby a decision is made is often as important as the decision itself." The open and free discussion between sometimes sharply opposing views is a model for political debate in a party and movement that advocate democracy. It may also be closer to reality than a single answer or policy. That is, a creative tension between points of view on the left may be more accurate and useful than the victory of one truth. A political party must of course adopt policy and draw lines between itself and other parties, and not all ideas can cohabit with one another. Yet there is something disturbing about the haste with which we on the left seek to close debate on issues. An open and tolerant process is useful for a political party. It is also useful for individuals. It serves to limit, even if it can never eliminate, the innate tendency in most of us to form, or borrow, a line on an issue, to delineate it from other lines, to wage war on behalf of our line, seeing our opponents as enemies, their arguments as specious and dangerous to progress. To admit my opponent is partly right is to admit that I might be partly wrong, a disturbing admission for most of us.

In my experience left-wing debates are often waged by that melodramatic manner, where victory is the order of the day, rather than by a dialectic, where exchanges can move us a step further in the search for creative change. In this debate the proponents of a new social contract heard both the practical difficulties of moving such a policy forward—you can read for yourself the intensity of the opposition—and substantial arguments against it: the belief by many trade unionists that collective bargaining is the workers' best defence, the likelihood of an incomes policy leading to increased centralization and bureaucracy, and the always present fear that such a social democratic reform will co-operate with and shore up the system socialists would like to replace. Yet the opponents of the proposed new social contract also heard substantive arguments: on the potential to give employees the degree of control they want in the workplace, on devising an incomes policy to protect the poor from inflation, on devising a party policy that offers not a perfect but the best way forward. Party politics after all is a struggle for victory in the here and now.

Because the debate was so open, the book is valuable as a kind of socialist reality therapy. Here are the tensions, the contradictions within the New Democractic Party. As Gerald Caplan concluded, "Within the NDP, as in almost every social democratic party in the world, the consensus has broken down". Nor had it broken down in these two days only on the issue of a new social contract. In fact the breakdown was nowhere more evident than in the sharp debate on the role of unions in the NDP that took place primarily in Session Two. There were also divisions over centralized vs. regional control, best illustrated in the debate between Garth Stevenson and Allan Blakeney, and between advocates of a pragmatic vs. a more long range and radical view of change. This last topic was the least well defined. The seminar not only permits the reader to understand issues on which debate has been well joined, but to see the outline of others that remain blurred. The place of the market in socialist thinking is obviously one such blurred issue. Richard Schwindt was the most explicit in defending its value, although even his was a qualified position. To me the debates feel like a place to start from—here are the divisions that exist. How do we now redefine socialism for the next decade?

That was a concern shared by all participants. Despite disagreements there was a deep level of consensus on two crucial matters: on the need to enunciate that clear new vision of socialism, and on the need for a new commitment to democracy. Elwood Cowley argued that at present the NDP's vision "has somehow either narrowed or vanished". Although he did not formulate a new vision, he longed to recreate the sense of confidence possessed by the Saskatchewan CCF when in power before 1964, with its vision of a comprehensive welfare state. Peter Warrian expressed the same idea: "The crucial questions for the left are not ones of policy, but how to create a vision and then the political agency to fulfil it." There were moments of such vision: Art Kube's desire for a society that pays more to day care workers than munitions workers, Leo Panitch's demand for a renewed socialist culture, Grant Notley's commitment to "the lived experience of people", and the misgiving shared by more than one speaker that today the right seems more the defender of the family and of the ordinary man than the left. Today the Progressive Conservatives may seem more democratic than the New Democrats to large portions of the Canadian population. The point was introduced by Leo Panitch and most sharply made by John Richards:

> A generation ago we in the CCF ... comfortably described ourselves with the slogan "humanity first", secure that we defended the values of ordinary men and women. Now, the right comfortably assumes the mantle of defender of the ordinary family while the left champions abortion on demand. We on the left support a "big state" and champion "big labour" in its conflicts with "big business". Many of the voices for the little guy's struggle against bigness come now from the right.

It was not the least virtue of this seminar to see this remarkable contradiction so clearly, and to recognize that a new vision of the left incorporating a new commitment to democracy is essential.

Of course everything in a seminar is a matter of words, and someone must have the last word. In this case it goes to Peter Warrian:

> For most of us our cultural references are literate, high culture. We rely too much on the written word; we express ourselves in a manner most people cannot understand, and we do social analysis based on information sources that are invisible or inaccessible to most people. But there is as much, or more knowledge about the economy in the bar at the Crown Point Hotel in Trail as in a university seminar room.

All the words in this seminar, and Peter Warrian's words and mine, are in the literate style of high culture. That was after all the audience. But democracy should mean more than new policies, structures or visions. It should mean new words, and learning as much from conversation at the Crown Point Hotel as from a book like this.

Introduction

John Richards

> In the summer of 1933 delegates assembled in Regina for the first national convention of the Co-operative Commonwealth Federation, the predecessor of the NDP. The ravages of the Great Depression had brought them together to form one party, with a determination to realize the "co-operative commonwealth", and prepared to compromise their self-interest to forge a common agenda of reform: the *Regina Manifesto*.
>
> Among these Canadians was an optimistic and defiant insistence that ordinary people—despite major divisions of region, ethnic origin and social class—could act together, democratically and independently of powerful "vested interests", to realize the common good....
>
> Now, fifty years later, we need to renew that Convention's sense of urgency, of commitment to fundamental change, and of willingness to act beyond narrow self-interest.
>
> *June 22nd Statement of Principles*

Grant Notley, leader of the Alberta NDP, died in October, 1984. He was flying, with nine other passengers and crew, aboard a small plane from Edmonton to his home town of Fairview, in his Peace River constituency. It was night; visibility was poor; the wings iced, and the plane crashed into the bush. Four survived; six died, including Grant.

The last time I saw Grant was two weeks earlier, at the wedding of a mutual friend. We ate and drank to the success of the marriage and—as we had done on many, many occasions—we indulged in a long rambling discussion on the future of the NDP. Assuming we both had years of active political life before us, we discussed ventures that were underway, and others that should be. A modest venture in the former category was this book, which has become, unfortunately, a testament to a dead friend.

The beginnings of this book were a seminar on the campus of the University of Alberta in May 1984, in a magnificent room overlooking the North Saskatchewan River. Grant played a central role in the events that led to this seminar, but before I proceed, let me give him a proper introduction.

Four times he was elected to the Alberta legislature by farmers and workers living in the small towns of one of Canada's most isolated ridings—in the northernmost corner of the Great Plains that stretch south to the Gulf of Mexico. Throughout Alberta's post-1973 oil boom the only elected Alberta socialist was Grant Notley. The voters in Canada's two fastest growing major cities declined to elect a single NDP member. Admittedly, in his last provincial election campaign (1982) voters in a working class riding in north Edmonton also elected Ray Martin, who has since become Grant's replacement as leader. That election doubled—from one to two—the NDP caucus, and Grant became Her Majesty's Leader of the Official Opposition. He frequently engaged in self-deprecating irony over his imposing title, but he genuinely relished the awesome task of his two-man dinghy attempting to sink the Conservative dreadnought. For someone ignorant of the role of rural people on the prairies in building Canadian socialism, and of the tendency of Alberta provincial voters to give overwhelming consensus support to their governing party, Grant's career must seem quixotic. For those who knew him, it was not quixotic at all. He was simply striving to give to urban people the vision of prairie socialism that had thrived in simpler rural communities.

An immodest task

Grant was modest in his personal political ambition, loyally devoted to his comrades within the Alberta NDP, and the federal party. Yet he undertook in the last years of his life a decidedly immodest task: to impose his vision of prairie socialism more forcefully upon the national New Democratic Party and, thereby, upon the national political culture. While he was too sophisticated to be accused of rural romanticism, too well-travelled to be labelled a narrow "provincial" politician, too sympathetic to working people's problems to be called "anti-labour", he nonetheless became decidedly impatient with a certain urban, centralizing, trade union centred vision that he felt was dominant in the federal New Democratic Party.

Despite his duties as Leader of the Opposition within the Alberta legislature he undertook, in the winter of 1982, to convene a group of his political "friends and allies" (including me) in order to "do something" about changing the federal NDP's agenda. Ultimately the tactic chosen was modest, to prepare a "counter-manifesto" to the "official manifesto" commissioned by the federal NDP Council. The latter document we found quite inadequate.

The year 1983 marked the fiftieth anniversary of the first national convention of the Co-operative Commonwealth Federation. Meeting in Regina in 1933, CCF delegates had adopted the *Regina Manifesto*. Despite its inadequacies when examined with the advantage of a half century of additional experience, it remains a fundamental document for Canadian socialists. In 1956 the CCF had adopted a more moderate manifesto, the *Winnipeg Declaration of Principles*, and at the NDP's 1961 founding convention delegates adopted the *New Party Declaration*. Over two decades had elapsed since the party had adopted a statement of principles and the fiftieth anniversary appealed to the NDP Council as an appropriate time for a new statement. Supporters of the "official manifesto" assumed it would be duly endorsed by delegates to the federal NDP convention, scheduled to meet in Regina in the summer of 1983.

When Grant first convened us, grey clouds and dirty snow enveloped Edmonton. By the time we had finished drafting our proclamation, the smell of fresh grass and the warmth of spring sunshine pervaded Grant's legislative offices. The day Grant Notley and Allan Blakeney released the document, at simultaneous news conferences in Calgary and Regina, was June 22nd. The document became the *June 22nd Statement of Principles*. At the beginning most of those Grant assembled were socialists whose roots were in the prairies. By the time the document was released, informal support for it had grown to include prominent NDP supporters across the country, including approximately a dozen NDP Members of Parliament.

Although it contained its fair share of political homilies, the document (reprinted as an appendix) made four important arguments. First was what might be termed the Jeffersonian argument that public participation in democratic politics required decentralization of political authority. While the document's argument was qualified—it also called for "a strong central government, strong enough to guarantee our national independence"—its thrust was to criticize the CCF/NDP tradition as having placed an excessive faith in the ability of central planners in Ottawa to solve problems. The document implicitly supported the Saskatchewan NDP position during the constitutional patriation debate, a position defending provincial rights so that provinces be able to act as laboratories for social change. It hinted at more radical ideas on decentralization: vastly increased powers to local and regional governments in the areas of social services and economic development. Second, the document made a generous offer to social democratic nationalists in Quebec, within and without the Parti Québécois. It admitted the extent to which the CCF/NDP had undervalued the "importance Québécois attached, and would continue to attach to the rights of their National Assembly as the guardian of francophone culture, and as an institution for the economic development of the only province in which French Canadians form a majority". Québécois had the right to opt for political independence, but hopefully they would not exercise the right because "(w)e firmly believe that the aspirations of Québécois are realizable with a new union which leaves important jurisdictions to a central government".

Third, the document unambiguously called for Canada to participate with other western democracies "in the collective defence of those liberties and freedoms people have fought for centuries, first, to acquire and, then, to retain". It evenhandedly condemned the military aggrandizement of both the Soviet Union and the United States.

Last, the document called for a new "social contract" on economic policy. Knowing this to be the most controversial passage, we drafted it with care. Rather than summarize what was already curt, let me quote:

> Now, as in the 1930s, the western industrial economies have suffered a serious economic crisis, and again the Right has argued that government intervention to improve economic performance would only make matters worse. To control inflation governments in the recent past, in Ottawa and other capitals, have pursued monetarist policies of restrictive credit and public spending. The result has been an immoral exchange: relative price stability at the cost of massive unemployment, particularly among the unskilled, the young, and the unprotected.

> We, in the NDP, restate our commitment that government must intervene aggressively to stimulate employment during difficult economic times.

> But government must also control inflation. At times, excess demand has been the cause, but in a society where powerful interests can set their prices, profits and incomes in terms of self-defined "fair shares", any economic shock that lowers the real income of some launches a dynamic of price-wage spiralling to "catch up". The only available alternative to

monetarism is income planning in key sectors. An incomes policy must be equitable: not a means to increase corporate profits at the expense of working people.

An incomes policy must figure as part of a larger agreement to create a new social contract in Canada. Such an agreement requires co-operation among government, labour and business. Among its major components must be a renewed commitment to full employment; government encouragement for workers to organize collectively, and to participate as equals in the management of the work place and the evaluation of new technology; better public accountability of government agencies and of Crown corporations; and development of new high-productivity sectors.

Why June 22nd?

Grant Notley spent most of his active career agitating to right the wrongs of political life within Alberta. He was content to let the scions of the federal NDP, most of whom were and are based in Ontario, determine NDP policy on matters of national concern. Such deference characterized many of us within the prairie NDP, and it required significant political events to convince us that our pragmatic vision of socialist potential needed to be argued on the national platform. What precipitated such a change? A minor factor was the humiliating electoral defeat inflicted on the Saskatchewan NDP in the 1982 provincial election. For the first time in over a decade, a cohort of prairie NDP leaders were no longer preoccupied by the problems of governing and turned their attention to national politics. Essentially, however, the change was the cumulative effect of three complex events: windfall resource benefits created by the commodity price boom of the 1970s, patriation of the constitution, and the post-1982 economic depression.

To review these events adequately would entail a separate and lengthy essay, but one can begin to understand the frustration of prairie socialists such as Grant by recalling the tenor of many past statements by federal spokesmen of the NDP on resources. They emphasized the problems posed by foreign-controlled oil companies seeking higher prices and profits at the expense of working class Canadian consumers; they argued for an assertion of federal power to maintain Canadian prices below world levels, and to redistribute oil rents out of the oil-producing provinces, Alberta in particular. If, out of deference for the NDP government in Saskatchewan, they did not say so explicitly, they implied that provincial resource rights were at best a legalistic irrelevancy to the central conflict, and at worst a manoeuvre of reactionary and co-opted provincial politicians. Certainly prairie New Democrats did not argue for provincial resource rights as an abstract exercise; we were well aware of the financial advantages to our constituents in such a position (just as New Democrats from Manitoba east were aware of the financial implications of their stance). Further we on the prairies were at times equivocal on the need for the federal government to redistribute resource rents and regulate powerful multinational oil companies. That said, the federal position offended the prairie socialist tradition. It showed no respect for historic struggles to assert local control over *all* resources—agricultural land as well as minerals. For socialists on the prairies the "enemy" has at times been external corporations such as Canadian Pacific in control of millions of acres of surface and subsurface rights; at times the "enemy" has been federal politicians of the "old line" parties perceived as puppets of these corporations. Now something of the same conflict existed inside the NDP.

The constitution patriation debate forced NDP politicians, at both the provincial and federal level, to address their divergences more clearly and publicly than many would have liked. In the fall of 1980 Ed Broadbent attempted—unsuccessfully—to pre-empt any internal party dissension by giving his immediate and unqualified endorsation as federal NDP leader to Prime Minister Trudeau's patriation resolution and entrenched charter of rights. As a concession he obtained from Trudeau a new section (92A) to the constitution. This section restored some of the provincial resource jurisdiction eroded by two Supreme Court constitutional decisions in which Saskatchewan's NDP government had been the loser. Despite this concession the Saskatchewan government, with the overwhelming support of its provincial party supporters, ultimately joined the provincial rights camp comprising eight of the provincial governments. With Ed Broadbent allied to Pierre Trudeau, and Allan Blakeney and Roy Romanow allied to Rene Levesque and Sterling Lyon, it was a time of strange beds and stranger bedfellows.

The issues at stake in the patriation debate were obviously more profound than who gets the windfall from rising oil and potash prices.

Even in the pragmatic political culture of Canada there arise moments when people are interested in the fundamental nature of democracy. Do Canadian socialists subscribe to the British Fabian tradition, in which effective social change depends primarily on reforms implemented by the cabinet and senior bureaucrats of the central govenment? Relative to claims of national unity or unity of class, how important are local and regional ties—ties that frequently cut across class and attenuate nationalist sentiments? Do we subscribe, and if so to what extent, to the radical Jeffersonian ideal that democracy is meaningful only where jurisdiction is subdivided to give the citizen opportunities to participate personally in public life? What are the appropriate roles for appointed judges relative to elected politicians in adjudicating conflicts over individual and collective rights?

In 1981 the gymnasium at the University of British Columbia campus in Vancouver provided the stage for one of the most dramatic public moments in the whole convoluted patriation process. Delegates to the federal New Democratic Party were assembled in convention. Some of the most eloquent speakers in Canadian politics and labour lined up to debate these questions at microphones strategically placed on the gymnasium floor. On the one side were Ed Broadbent, Stanley Knowles, Dave Barrett and—a disappointment for us—Tommy Douglas; on the other were Allan Blakeney, Roy Romanow, Grant Notley, Reg Baskin (then head of the Alberta Federation of Labour) and Lorne Nystrom. By a margin of roughly five to three the nationalist "Jacobins" dominated the populist "Girondins", but the dilemmas continued to gnaw at many New Democrats, including Grant.

The third event has been the post-1982 economic depression. Was there a link between Canada's entry into what proved to be the country's worst depression since the 1930s and opinion poll results revealing falling popular support for the NDP? Relentlessly support fell until, in the spring of 1984, polls gave the NDP the support of fewer than half the Canadians prepared to support the party two years earlier. NDP politicians, like all contemporary politicians, follow polls fervently, and the decline gave an urgency to Grant and those of us close to him who were convinced that such a link existed. (The results of the 1984 election gave us a quick lesson in the danger of simple explanations in politics. Due in part to the calibre of the federal NDP campaign, due in part to the incompetence of John Turner who alienated left wing Liberal voters and chased them to the NDP, NDP support rebounded. The party's popular vote declined only marginally between the 1980 and 1984 elections.)

Those of us around Grant reluctantly came to believe that the Canadian public was—at least partially—correct to reject us at this time. Canadians, we concluded, want New Democrats around during inflationary times as a lobby for equity in social programs. Canadians do not think us competent to manage an industrial economy and, in particular, to restore full employment in a depressed economy. At the risk of imposing too much order on many free-wheeling economic discussions, let me try to summarize.

People had been legitimately concerned about inflation and yet we in the NDP had no consistent solution. Federal NDP leaders rightly condemned the burden of unemployment created by pursuit of monetarism as a solution to inflation, but they refused to endorse, even in principle, the only other basic solution—resort to an incomes policy. We were uneasy about the confidence placed by party leaders in advocating Keynesian fiscal stimulus as a guaranteed cure for high unemployment.[1] Federal NDP spokesmen slipped rather too easily from making the legitimate case for government planning via an "industrial strategy" into advocacy of permanent protection for low productivity manufacturing jobs. They attacked the undeniable problems of open markets and international trade and extolled the virtues of Canadian economic independence, implicitly denigrating the export-oriented resource economy of western Canada as mere "hewing of wood and drawing of water". Without ignoring the human costs of dislocating people from existing jobs, we were convinced the NDP must construct a more forceful response from the left on issues of productivity and comparative advantage in international trade. Nationalization of firms under present poor labour-management relations was certainly not the solution.

Common to many of our arguments was a conviction that collective bargaining in Canada has not been working well, and that we in the NDP have an obligation to explore alternatives that entail workers collectively assuming more responsibility for management, with consequently less reliance on adversarial collective bargaining. We summarized all these imprecise ideas as the need for a new "social contract" between workers, capitalists and government. No such social contract could hope to secure worker support, we realized, unless it also enhanced the ability of workers to undertake collective bargaining. One cannot pursue economic policy very far in the NDP without addressing the organic link between the party and the organized labour movement. We knew that. We hoped, however, to launch the debate on a "social contract" without precipitating the opposition of labour leaders in the party. In retrospect, it was a naive hope. Given the extensive experience that we as prairie socialists have had with individually owned enterprises in the case of farming, of co-operatives and of provincial crown corporations, it came naturally to us to envision changes to present collective bargaining practices. But for virtually all union leaders legislation enabling collective bargaining is their Magna Carta, and it approaches heresy for supporters of the NDP to discuss alternatives or constraints on it. Except in Saskatchewan and, to a lesser extent, Manitoba and British Columbia, trade unionists do not perceive the NDP as a potential government. They see their own union struggles as paramount, and are reluctant to compromise significantly their interests to permit realization of a potential majority coalition behind the NDP. Indeed many labour leaders close to the NDP expect the party to give uncritical support to labour's position, to act as a counter to the anti-labour bias of much public debate.

The group around Grant shared what might best be termed a left-populist perspective. We conceived organized labour as an essential component of a left alliance. But, if it is to be credible as an agent of "all the people", the NDP must define policy independently of any special interest group, even interest groups with which we are in alliance. An alternative "labour party" perspective baulks at any consideration of organized labour as an interest group comparable to others. Indeed, by this perspective, it is the organic link of a political party to the union movement that gives it socialist legitimacy.

After June 22nd

If our purpose as authors of the *June 22nd Statement* was to enliven what augured to be a dull convention—a 50th birthday for a middle-aged party mired in third place—we succeeded brilliantly! If our purpose was to impose a new vision on the federal NDP, we made but a very modest beginning.

We cannot complain that our document went unnoticed. It received wide media attention and discussion among party members. However those in the federal leader's office and in certain union headquarters were "not amused" when, one week prior to its publication, they learned of this major counter-manifesto supported by prominent party leaders. To some extent they feared history repeating itself. Prior to the 1969 federal convention a group of prominent New Democrats had released the *Waffle Manifesto*, as a left nationalist critique of the party. The 1969 convention debate over that manifesto catalyzed half a decade of inner party conflict. Those in the leader's office ardently wanted to avoid an analogous potentially divisive open debate between supporters of the two documents.

As a gesture of goodwill supporters of the *June 22nd Statement* ultimately acquiesced to a compromise whereby the two manifestos were amalgamated. Many delegates were understandably disappointed that a "backroom deal" had been struck. The resulting "cut and paste" manifesto (as its critics dubbed it) included more or less intact the *June 22nd* text on decentralization and Quebec, but it expunged all mention of a social contract. Predictably the amalgamated document was endorsed by the convention, but without great enthusiasm. It lacked the legitimacy it would have enjoyed had it emerged as the result of open debate on the convention floor.

* * *

All that serves as prologue to explain why forty people assembled in the spring of 1984 on the bank of the North Saskatchewan River to debate a new social contract. Many, on all sides of the issue, wanted a forum in which discussion could be joined.

---

[1] Here we anticipated by six months the arguments made by James Laxer upon resigning as research director of the federal NDP caucus. See J. Laxer, *Rethinking the Economy* (Toronto: NC press, 1984).

Session One: The Culture of Politics

A Social Contract or Socialism?

Leo Panitch

I read with interest the *June 22nd Statement of Principles*, and while I think it a welcome venture, I strongly disagree with much of it—in particular its advocacy of an incomes policy. As overture to my critique, I want to discuss the contemporary popularity of conservative "market populism".

The first lesson the current situation teaches is that there is nothing automatic about the development of socialist consciousness—whether reformist or revolutionary. There is nothing automatic about it even when the capitalist economy fails to generate material benefits or job security for working people. In the absence of effective organization, of popular language, of concrete support, and of meaningful program, the impact of the socialist may be no greater when the capitalist and his political henchmen are calling for restraints and sacrifice than when they were able to proclaim "you never had it so good".

This does not mean we give up. On the contrary, it demonstrates the urgency of new socialist initiatives. The urgency becomes more apparent every day in light of the onslaught we are facing and the failure of the left in its present state to provide an adequate defence, let alone a basis for socialist advance.

In the Canadian context we must first understand exactly why the NDP is not currently gaining substantial new electoral support. I do not want to debate whether the polls are currently (spring 1984) wrong to put federal NDP support at 13%, or whether it is really 20%. What is astonishing from our perspective is—why it is not 50%. This is not the time to say—as many from my ideological perspective have often said—that the NDP is not really socialist, that it betrays the working class by advocating tepid reform rather than revolution, that it co-opts the working class rather than mobilizing to overthrow the capitalist state. We must ask, rather, why, given the inadequacies of the right, do people not at least prefer the NDP's reformism as a political strategy? There are various explanations for this.

One explanation lies in the superficial, but prevalent, response to the crisis which blames the government of the day, and supports the major opposition party. A second and more fundamental explanation is that the NDP's failure to generate and develop socialist consciousness in the period of economic growth has laid the basis for its further failure in the period of depression. Reforms may actually gather support when the capitalist system appears able to support them. They may lose that support when the fear of unemployment and the onslaught against previous reforms gain the upper hand, thus demonstrating how utterly dependent our system, our governments and all of us are on meeting the conditions that capitalists set as to when and where they will invest. Insofar as workers understand, as I think they do, the logic of capitalism and insofar as the NDP's reformism implicitly accepts that logic, many people rightly fear that the NDP will scare business away—even before the Liberals and Conservatives tell them so.

But even this is a limited explanation for it ignores the real resonance which conservative, anti-statist, market-populist ideology has for many working people. The NDP, in the post-war period, has taken credit for expansion of the Keynesian/welfare capitalist state. The solution the NDP offers to the current crisis involves a defence of this state and a call for further expansion of it. However, the Keynesian promise to overcome permanently boom and bust in the capitalist economy is now being proven false. Except for some Marxists, most of the left used to walk around saying a depression would not happen again. But the fact that Keynesianism has been proven a failure in predicting the ability to maintain full employment at stable prices is not the main point. More important, the Keynesian/welfare state is, to some extent, deservedly unpopular in the eyes of many Canadians. It is often bureaucratic, often inefficient and, above all, it is distant from popular control in any meaningful sense of the term.

As socialists we know this critique applies all the more to the large bureaucratic private corporation. But the lack of popular control in the private sector does not deny the significance of its lack in the public sector. When we criticize government as distant, that is as true for the workers employed by government as for the clients using government services. The word "public" - whether applied to enterprise, to employees, to service—has become a dirty word in Canadian political culture during the last decade. This change is, in part, the result of a barrage of denigration by businessmen, politicians and journalists. It is an aspect of a right wing strategy that involves turning the screws on workers, women, and the poor. But we must acknowledge that this critique is often echoed by those very groups because it articulates their experience of alienation from government.

For the NDP, or any other party, currently to advocate the expansion of public expenditure, or even the exercise of public control over private expenditure, is a recipe for electoral disaster. It is ironic and unfair that the NDP, the party that has had the least direct control over the Canadian state, should be the most associated in the popular imagination with the undesirable aspects of the state. But it is understandable that this should be so. The NDP has always insisted that, without its pressure, post-war expansion of the role of the state would not have occurred. And to some extent NDP leaders are correct in this claim.

It is also symptomatic of the NDP that its leaders continue to insist that the Keynesian/welfare state is a little bit pregnant with socialism, that its expansion is part of a long gradual process towards socialism. All that is needed is a further gestation period. But it is strategically mistaken, I think, to say that welfare state reforms, Keynesian fiscal policy, and crown corporations represent a way station on the highway to democratic socialism. It is clearly not true; these reforms are being repealed today. It is also tactically disastrous today, even for a reformist party like the NDP, to seek support by defending expansion of an unchanged state, given how it is currently structured and perceived.

For socialists it is a grave source of concern that a right-wing market populism has rushed in to fill the vacuum left by the demise of liberal or social democratic ideology. This right-wing populism articulates some of the most blatantly reactionary elements of capitalist ideology to have surfaced in political debate in some time. Its success underlies the urgency of our getting our act together. But we must learn from the current mood and appreciate how it opens up new possibilities for us.

The monetarist assault and the failure of Keynesianism should not be the occasion for a defence of the existing state. They provide the opportunity to propose the fundamental democratic restructuring of the state so that the communities it serves and the people who work for it can both achieve greater direct involvement and control over it. Rather than the debate over a bigger or smaller state, we have to recognize that antipathy to the state can be addressed in the old socialist way—by speaking of a *different kind of state*.

We must also recognize that neoconservatism/market populism is not only a rational capitalist strategy for increasing the rate of exploitation. It also seeks to reinforce many traditional values, of patriarchy and capitalism, values which feminists, political reformers and trade unionists have all sought to modify. These values have retained a strong basis in popular culture, a basis we have been unable to shake. For many in our society, in different classes, the terms "individualism", "the family", "thrift", "competitiveness", "a woman's place is in the home", "right to life", have a positive connotation.

Market populism or neoconservatism gains its purchase as ideology not only because it addresses public policies, such as the deficit, taxation and wage restraint, but because it also addresses how people should live their private lives. Now the propagation of these values has a retrograde effect. It seems to me they reinforce the atomization and isolation of people in this economic crisis. But these values "work" because they do provide moral guidance and create a sense of community, however false. People can and do identify themselves, and each other, by recourse to these traditional values.

All of this carries for socialists, contemplating how to begin anew, lessons that amount to a rediscovery of some of the most basic socialist principles. The first is that our political alternatives must not only solve unemployment, control investment and provide services, important as those are, they must also make viable the exercise of popular control over the state and capital. We must project a new form of democracy. The failure to do this is one of the great failures of both Marxists and social democrats. Marxists have tended to think that, once you take over the means of production, political administration was a minor detail. Social democrats have tended to think you could take over the existing state and humanize it, and not think much about the fundamentally required political institutions for a socialist society. We are suffering badly from those failures.

Against two false notions—that an individual can overcome his insecurity and hopelessness by pulling him/herself up by the bootstraps, or that a distant bureaucratic state will solve our problems for us—we must project a socialism that provides a means for popular participation in economic and social planning at all levels, at the level of industry and local community as well as at regional and national levels. We must advance new institutional arrangements at every level of society.

At the same time we must understand our practice to be cultural as well as political. One of the clearest lessons of working class history is that the successful building of mass socialist parties and of trade unions entails bringing to life alternative communities. The successful party or union becomes the centre of a vibrant cultural milieu of schools, pubs, theatres, as well as co-operative health and retail centres. In Canada there is presently an evident separation between, on the one hand, the NDP, primarily an electoral and resolution-passing machine, and the unions, primarily collective bargaining agents, and, on the other hand, broader cultural life. The present stands in sharp contrast to the integrative role between culture and politics which the labour temples, for example, used to play. Unless we can create vibrant socialist communities which stand as a living testament to the liberating potential of socialism, socialist politics are destined to be at best marginal and at worst alien and threatening to Canadians.

The limits of social democratic "social contracts"

In the light of the above discussion, and only in this light, ought we to talk about the adequacy of any social contract, and about the potential of a new social contract to deliver socialism from its present impasse. I want now to turn to the main question of this conference—the compatibility between socialism and some new social contract. For a number of reasons I think this initiative welcome. It represents the search for new strategic direction, something clearly important to us. It recognizes that the call for increased public expenditure will by itself not suffice. It recognizes, third, that the new right has a resonance with the public because it addresses real problems, among them working people's fear of inflation.

At the centre of the new social contract approach is the call for an incomes policy, some form of agreement from unions to accept wage restraint and from corporations to accept price or profit constraint. The call for an incomes policy comes from two sources. It comes first from those who conclude that increasing employment by a more aggressive fiscal policy will accelerate inflation, and so workers must sacrifice to prevent this consequence. As Hugh Scanlon (head of the British engineering workers' union) once put it, it is an appeal that we cut our heads off ourselves rather than have someone else do it for us. It comes also from those, such as Jim Laxer,[1] who argue that Canadians must play the international competitive game on capitalists' terms, one element of which, in addition to rapid adoption of new "high tech" industries, is wage restraint.

In my view an incomes policy is exactly the wrong way to go. As the case for it is argued, the "social contract" has an anachronistic ring to it. It sounds like a charge backward to the 1960s. It is a borrowing from the past practice of European social democratic parties, a borrowing of something which has largely proved to be a failure and which socialist parties are currently trying to transcend.

The most spectacular failure of a social democratic social contract was that of the last Labour government in Britain. As in 1947-48 and 1964, the 1974-79 Labour government struck a social contract with the trade unions. The unions agreed to voluntary wage restraint in exchange for certain reforms: temporary price controls, some significant additions to legislated trade union powers, etc. The unions co-operated. Usually such social contracts are criticized as unworkable because of the bloody mindedness of unions. Wrong! European union leaders have gone out of their way to co-operate with social democratic governments in extensive wage restraint programs. These social contracts prove unworkable because the other side of the bargain is often not met. Certainly British Labour governments did not deliver, neither under Prime Minister Wilson after 1964 nor under Prime Ministers Wilson and Callaghan after 1974. Price controls were quickly abandoned under pressure from financial interests in the City of London and from the International Monetary Fund. Many of the other social reforms promised were not introduced; what remained was wage control. As Labour budgets came to reflect monetarist dictates on the need for public sector restraint, low paid workers suffered most. (Among the first of western capitalist governments to introduce monetarism was the British under a Labour prime minister, "Sunny Jim" Callaghan.) In the winter of 1978-79 the incomes policy broke down in a wave of strikes, primarily of low paid public sector workers.

We are not here talking of the "British disease". The problem is general. We are subject in Canada to myth-making about West Germany and Japan. The much vaunted West German social contract lasted a year and a half. Introduced in 1967, it was over by 1969. It collapsed due to government inability to fulfil its commitments and consequent union bitterness. Since then there has been no effective union participation in German incomes policy, and the unions formally pulled out in 1978.

Admittedly a social democratic social contract has worked in certain countries: in Austria, Sweden and Norway. But even in Sweden we have seen a breakdown. The Swedish Social Democrats, who have since been re-elected, suffered defeat in 1976. Prior to this defeat massive strikes occurred against the social contract, amidst union accusations that it had frozen the distribution of income. Unions began demanding public control of investment, and in exchange for further wage restraint, they demanded a "wage earners' fund" whereby the unions would obtain majority equity control of major firms. Olaf Palme's Social Democrats have accepted the principle of the wage earners' fund but have stretched its implementation to such an extent that, by my calculations, it will require 280 years. Even in Scandinavia a social democratic social contract has not prevented the ravages of the international economic crisis. It may have softened the impact—undeniably the social wage is higher there—but current unemployment is high by Scandinavian, especially Swedish, standards. Even in Austria, from where I have just returned, unemployment exceeds 5% and social tensions are enormous.

Why do social democratic social contracts break down? They collapse because, as trade unionists constantly tell politicians, they are inequitable in practice. They tend to freeze the distribution of income; they tend to hurt the low paid most; they tend to be primarily wage restraint. At the centre of every social democratic social contract has been wage restraint. This generalization is more true in Britain; it is admittedly less true of some other social democratic administrations. Now I do not oppose wage restraint under all circumstances. Indeed any socialist party spearheading a popular attack on the power of the corporate elite would be dishonest or naive not to make clear to its working class supporters that even the parliamentary road to socialism entails considerable material sacrifice and bitter struggle at every level of society. Without this understanding the electorate will abandon a socialist government at the first moment of strong capitalist resistance.

But the call for a social democratic social contract is something else. It is part of the attempted redefinition of socialism by elements of social democratic parties over the past forty years in terms of Keynesian theories of sustained expansion within a capitalist economy. For these elements the central dilemma is the existence of a tradeoff, as an economy approaches full employment, between expansion of aggregate demand and inflationary pressure. The resulting inflation may arise due to demand pressures—too much money chasing too few goods and bidding up prices—or supply pressure—the working class under conditions of near full employment increasing wages and capitalists responding by increasing prices. This is a real dilemma in the eyes of Keynesians.

Why, we might ask, is inflation a problem? It is obviously a problem for single mothers and pensioners on fixed incomes. But why is it also a problem for capitalists? Wage pressure tends to undermine profits, and in Keynesian theory the whole purpose of demand stimulation, however done, is to induce capitalists to reinvest a higher proportion of their profits. If stimulation of demand leads to domestic inflation, the country's goods will rise in price relative to those of other countries, export demand will fall, and with it domestic profits. Currency devaluation, price controls, import and exchange controls will not necessarily solve the problem of a negative balance of payments; they may simply disrupt competitive markets and destroy business confidence on which the economy depends. Unless such measures are combined with effective wage restraint, the economy will stagnate at a high unemployment level with low profits. In response social democratic Keynesians call for an incomes policy in the context of a social contract. It is a capitalist logic.

When in government, sincere social democrats introduce social contracts involving incomes policies with the best of intentions that they be equitable. Why does it turn out that they are inequitable? Let me answer with two examples. The politicians usually promise that low paid workers will benefit most from an incomes policy. They argue that unconstrained collective bargaining is a system in which the strong benefit and the weak go to the wall. They proceed to set a 10% limit on annual wage increases for the low paid, and 5% for the well paid. But how do you transfer profits from a high wage industry, such as oil refining, to a low wage industry, such as textiles? How are the wage costs saved in the one to be passed to capitalists in the other in order for them to pay higher wages? Textile employers do not pay low wages because they are ogres; they operate on low profit margins in general and could not pay much more without facing bankruptcy. How to effect that transfer has frustrated almost every experience of an incomes policy, with the exception of the Swedes'. Through "solidarity wage bargaining" in a highly centralized union federation, Swedish unions have secured high wages across the board, letting low productivity firms go bankrupt. Furthermore the Swedish government mounts an extensive manpower program to retrain workers for expanding industries. That works so long as capital is expanding. When it is not, as at present, the Swedish manpower program serves mainly to keep workers off the unemployment lists.

I want to address two additional problems with respect to a social democratic social contract. I find it astonishing that those calling for it are those within the NDP who appreciate most the left populist tradition of the prairies. Social democratic social contracts are elitist centralized arrangements, even in the most successful cases. This is certainly true of Austria where the leaders of highly undemocratic, highly centralized trade unions meet behind closed doors, usually the closed doors of the socialist party. This collaboration admittedly does produce a marginally more equitable society than in either Britain or Canada, but it is certainly far from populist. If you speak to people in countries with well-established social contracts, they talk about dissipation of popular participation in their socialist parties, about the serious problem of them being no longer centres of socialist culture.

Second, we should recognize the deleterious effect that the language of the social contract has on political discourse in this country. Leaders of the NDP, and of the CCF before it, have always been sensitive that they, unlike so many self-proclaimed revolutionaries, have understood the need to speak the indigenous popular language. As David Lewis put it, it is impossible to persuade people to an idea, especially a new one, if one uses words and concepts which close their minds; they may continue to listen politely, but they do not hear a thing. On the basis of this fundamental insight the CCF in the 1940s undertook not an adaptation of socialist thought to Canadian conditions but a project of reassurance to Canadians that the CCF was not socialist after all. CCF leaders appropriated Mackenzie King's World War II slogan ("conscription if necessary, but not necessarily conscription") for their own purposes saying, in effect, "socialism if necessary, but not necessarily socialism". You cannot change political discourse with that kind of ambiguity. Bernard Shaw once said that a Chekhov or Shakespeare can make a comedy or tragedy of indecision, but even they cannot turn it into a clarion call. When CCF leaders discovered people were afraid of bank nationalization because they did not know what would happen to their deposits—a legitimate concern—they dropped the plank from the program. (The Canadian Labour Congress has just resurrected it.) When they discovered people were afraid of public ownership—not surprising when they looked at Eastern Europe—CCF leaders rephrased their policy as "public ownership if necessary, but not necessarily public ownership". This is an easy, but unimaginative way to reassure people, and ultimately it is self-defeating. By resorting to it, the NDP cannot explain how exploitation is inherent in the private ownership of the means of production, and must sacrifice the vision of democratic worker or community control of enterprise to a notion of state regulation of private enterprise. We adopt a Keynesian mixed economy language, one the Liberals can easily steal. They are good at that language; it permits them to be everything to everybody.

The language of the social contract also poses these problems. It creates a myth of big labour and big capital solving the country's problems on a basis of equality. An absurdity! Sure, in a formal sense an individual worker who contracts with his employer does so on a basis of equality. But that formal equality masks a substantive inequality. Similarly under a social democratic social contract a formal equality exists between central federations of labour and capital; both have equal numbers at the negotiating table. But there exists enormous inequality in financial, ideological and political resources between them. Talk of a social contract feeds a myth of equality.

In conclusion, do we ignore inflation? No. One of our mistakes has been to call for increased public expenditure without concern for the legitimate fear of ensuing inflation. Usually we rule out price controls as an answer to inflation; I am unsure why. In most effective social contracts, above all in Austria, they are present. With selective subsidies, it is possible to impose them in an open economy such as ours. I make two points in favour of price over wage controls. It is one thing to control a commodity; it is qualitatively different to control a human being. Second, who buys the pig in the poke? With wage controls the worker hopes that inflation will not erode the value of his constrained wages; he assumes the risk. With price controls the capitalist must hope; he takes the risk.

If we are to rebuild our economic base—a legitimate goal—let us not play the Keynesian game that disguises and supports the capitalist system. Let us consider, for instance, the CLC's program of bank nationalization. To be sure this program poses a problem, that with which I began, the current unpopularity of the state. How can we speak of price controls and bank nationalization given the unpopularity of state intervention? I therefore end with this admonition. We should not play around with social contracts, but instead address the redefinition and rediscovery of the nature of socialist democratic political institutions. Rather than sitting behind closed doors elaborating arrangements for wage restraint, we should open a public debate on democratic socialism.

---

¹See his recent essay: J. Laxer, *Rethinking the Economy* (Toronto: NC Press, 1984).

The Art of the Possible

Elwood Cowley

My contribution to the discussion of a new social contract is to consider the potential for a social democratic government to intervene in the community. I will look at our experience as the government of Saskatchewan in introducing two programs that reflected fundamentally our social democratic politics: the land bank and nationalization of part of the potash industry. I will try to explain how members of the NDP conceived them, how we tried to administer them as a government, how the public received them, and how they did or did not change the nature of society in Saskatchewan.

In conclusion I will comment briefly on what Leo Panitch said, and state my sense of what is desirable in a social contract between unions and the NDP. Leo and I are two trains going in somewhat different directions. We are, fortunately, on separate tracks and will avoid a head-on collision.

The Land Bank

The debate about the land bank began in the Saskatchewan NDP in the late 1960s, and it was very lively. At the time some people had organized a ginger group in the party called the "Waffle", and they introduced the issue. It became a significant issue of debate primarily because of the state of agriculture at the time. Farmers wanting to retire were having trouble selling land at what they felt were reasonable prices. Young people who wanted to enter farming had great difficulty finding credit to purchase land. How could we in the NDP "save the family farm"? In particular, how could we provide for transfer from father to son?

The idea of the land bank was simple but radical. The government should buy land from farmers wanting to sell, and rent it to farmers wanting land to farm. Debate in the party in 1970 and 1971 centred on a specific aspect, whether to include for farmers renting land an option to purchase at some future date. Those who supported the option to purchase, roughly the anti-Waffle element of the party, argued that we could not get elected without it. That was a fairly telling argument!

There were a lot of people in the NDP wanting to get elected, myself included. I was running as a candidate in Biggar, a rural riding west of Saskatoon. The Waffle supporters who argued against the option to purchase thought of the land bank as the beginning of an alternative to the private market in land. With the option to purchase the program would simply be a band-aid solution. It's pointless, they argued, to buy the land from the father, rent it to the son, and then let the son buy it if that looks financially attractive at a time of rising farm prices. You would wind up buying it from the son to rent to the grandson, and would have done nothing to eliminate speculation in farm land. As well, with no option to purchase, administering the plan would be a lot easier; you would avoid the problem of capital gains and losses as land prices went up or down. While I didn't agree at the time with the Waffle position, and still don't, running the programme would have been much simpler without the option to purchase. A third argument was, what happens when we're not the government anymore? If farmers had leased land, would a Liberal government take their land away and sell it to their political friends? Indeed, the present Conservative government has, essentially, forced farmers to buy their rented land or give it up.

Although it never surfaced much at the time, and we paid little attention to it, many people, even people within the NDP, opposed in principle state ownership of land.

Despite its pitfalls, there was obviously a lot of public support for the land bank idea and we needed a program to deal with the land transfer problem. So we ran with the land bank as part of the 1971 election program:

> The continuing degradation of Saskatchewan agriculture and the related decline of our rural communities are the most critical issues before the people of the province....

> It is time to take a stand. The New Democratic Party rejects the capitalist economic doctrine that human values must be sacrificed if they stand in the way of technology and "efficiency"....

> As first steps, an NDP government will .... establish a Land Bank Commission which could purchase land offered voluntarily on the market at competitive prices and lease this land, guaranteeing tenure, on the basis of need, with option to buy, with the objective of promoting the maximum number of viable family farms in Saskatchewan....[1]

Nobody noticed it; nobody cared; they were too busy trying to get rid of the unpopular Liberal government, headed by Ross Thatcher. So we got through the 1971 election campaign without raising much controversy over the land bank. The booklet, New Deal for People, had 200 programs in it. During the next four years we dutifully checked them off as we implemented them—including the land bank. As a government we put a lot of effort into the land bank as a program.

When we started buying land for the land bank, there was no lack of farmers willing to sell to the government. There weren't many others to sell to. Fathers were quite happy to sell their land to us since we guaranteed it could be rented by their sons. Father had his money and headed for Arizona; son carried on farming. We didn't organize the program as a subsidy to farmers, but initial rents were reasonably low because we were able to buy initially at reasonably low prices. It all ran very nicely. But there were some farmers selling to us who had no children wanting to rent the land. We set up a board to decide which deserving farmer would receive the land; we even had an appeal board. We bought a section of land, put it up for lease and thirty-two aspiring young farmers—all from my constituency—applied to rent it. (Actually only thirty-one considered themselves deserving. After a few drinks the thirty-second admitted he wasn't.) Only one could receive it. At this point we began to notice some difficulties in the program. But being dedicated socialist politicians, we carried on. We didn't know what else to do! By and large we administered it fairly. We devised an elaborate point system to determine who rented the available land, and the people working for the Land Bank Commission were pretty straightforward. There was no political patronage. But that turned out to be a political problem too. No one was impressed when the local Tory got land. New Democrats were mad, and Tories wouldn't vote for us anyway. As for the option to purchase, we said that farmers on rented land could buy after five years, provided they arranged their financing somewhere else and paid us outright. We didn't want the land bank to become a source of mortgage money for buying land.

By 1975, when we called the next election, we had done a lot of hard work on the land bank, and other programs. Despite our work the land bank hit the fan, as the saying goes. "This could well be the most important provincial election ever to face the people of Saskatchewan," warned the Liberals. "The issue is very clear: more and more government control of our lives by a power-hungry NDP Socialist Government or greater freedom of choice, independence and long-range prosperity under a new Liberal Government." They went on:

> It is becoming increasingly clear to Saskatchewan residents, especially farmers, that the Land Bank is not a transfer system, but a method by which the NDP seek to implement a landlord system of farming under which the farmers are merely tenants of the government. Another term of office for the NDP will mean an alarming increase in the number of state farms in Saskatchewan.[2]

The Liberals decided to make the land bank *the* issue. In defending the program we found ourselves forced into defending state ownership of farm land all over the province. Attacking state ownership was their best argument, the one hardest to counter. Remember, they would say, that your parents and grandparents left the Ukraine, or wherever, to get away from government owning all the land and look what these damn socialists are doing to you. You might as well have stayed in the Ukraine. You got one good generation in here and those Bolsheviks caught up with you. We felt a little defensive during the campaign but, thanks to a split in the opposition vote between the Liberals and born-again Tories, we won the election. The Liberals fell from 43% in 1971 to 32%; the Tories, who were dead in 1971 with only 2% of the vote, got 28% this time. We got 39 of 61 seats, but we got only 40% of the vote, the lowest percentage since 1938 and 15% below our 1971 result. We had lost two elections in the 1960s with a higher popular vote. Clearly something was astir out there and we, thinking we had done such a good job, were a little surprised and disappointed.

The process by which the land bank policy emerged was a good one. There was a vigorous debate in the party; the party supported the policy, and we told the electorate what we were going to do. But we were still caught out—partly by the upturn in the farm economy after 1972. By the 1975 election land prices had started to go up, the banks were loaning money again, and people were less interested in the land bank. And the guys who got land from the land bank two years earlier (their fathers having sold it at the then princely sum of $100/acre to the government) were now looking at land across the road selling at $175/acre and thinking it's going to be three years before they could exercise their option to buy, and by that time prices might be $200/acre (actually prices were more like $500/acre in 1978). What am I going to do about this? these guys said to themselves.

We carried on with the land bank through to our defeat in 1982, but I think—and this is a personal opinion—the land bank never became a popular program except with the successful lessees, and the left wingers in the NDP who liked the concept of public land ownership. It did not make a lasting social or economic change in Saskatchewan. Once the economic squeeze of 1969-71 ended, the land bank became the focal point of protracted political opposition. It was criticized—unfairly—for driving land prices up. It alienated 31 of 32 applicants, all except the successful one. It remains today an important philosophical and practical problem for Saskatchewan New Democrats. What do we say now when someone asks, what are you going to do with the land bank when you are re-elected? (Despite the licking we got in 1982, some people actually think we will be re-elected!) We have no answer yet to that question.

Potash Nationalization

My second example is potash. We had been elected, in 1971 and again in 1975, with a statement in small print in our program that we would greatly increase public ownership in the resource sector. We promised to:

> oppose any further sellout of our resources. With respect to new development, the NDP will give first priority to public ownership through crown corporations. Co-operative ownership will be encouraged. Partnership arrangements between government and co-operatives or private developers will be undertaken when appropriate. Limits will be established with respect to foreign equity capital, and every effort will be made to limit foreign investment in resource development to non-equity capital.[3]

On potash we promised to:

> end the present (Liberal) government collaboration in a potash cartel that restricts Saskatchewan output and jobs. Because the present owners have generally shown unconcern about jobs for Saskatchewan miners, and because they have used their power to force farmers to pay exorbitant fertilizer prices, an NDP government will consider the feasibility of bringing the potash industry under public ownership.[4]

These were little more than statements, certainly not well debated programs like the land bank. We snuck them into the program in 1971.

Between 1971 and 1975 we introduced Saskoil, a publicly owned crown oil company which didn't create much of a furore. We also created a crown mineral exploration company which was busy in northern Saskatchewan looking for uranium, and we found a major uranium deposit. (People in the NDP thought uranium was just another mineral at that time.) As we were working quietly on these projects, we were having considerable difficulty with the potash people. As agricultural markets improved in 1972, fertilizer prices rose dramatically and the potash companies started making handsome profits. In 1974 we introduced a major new tax, the potash reserve tax, to get some of that revenue for the government. Between 1973 and 1975 we increased government potash revenues by a factor of ten—from about $10 million annually to $100 million. In the 1975 election we tried to make potash an issue, saying that the companies were failing to expand production and increase jobs, and that they weren't willing to pay their fair share of taxes. But people weren't interested. As it turned out, they were more interested in the land bank.

After the election the cabinet met. This is a personal view but I think that, although we had won the election, we thought it had been a defeat. Why? The Liberals had collapsed, but votes we had expected had gone to the Tories. As I said, they went from nothing in 1971 to over a quarter of the vote. It was frustrating. The Tories had cocky new MLAs sitting opposite us in the legislature. They were the first Tories in the Saskatchewan legislature since Martin Pederson, the lone Tory elected in 1964. It was the first time there had been more than one (they elected seven in 1975) since 1934, before I was born. We looked around and asked, what are we going to do?

Shortly before the election, we had created the Potash Corporation of Saskatchewan (PCS), a crown corporation. At the time we hadn't decided what its role would be in the potash industry. Within two weeks of the election, the potash companies took us to court. In part inspired by a constitutional challenge by the oil industry to our oil royalty legislation, they challenged our right to impose the potash reserve tax. They already had another case going that challenged our right as a government to regulate potash production, and they launched two or three more cases to make our life miserable. We decided in cabinet to nationalize the industry, using PCS. Obviously there were ideological reasons for doing so. Some in cabinet and caucus thought it a great idea, whatever the problems. Others thought it an effective tactic in the conflict over resource revenues. We can fix those potash companies. They aren't paying the reserve tax and are taking us to court to challenge our right to tax. If we take over the mines and run them ourselves, there will be no question of potentially unconstitutional taxation. Finally, we had spent four year working extremely hard to introduce an elaborate set of programs which the electorate didn't really appreciate, so some thought let's do something *we* would like to do.

No one in cabinet deluded themselves that potash nationalization would be a popular move, at least initially. We didn't take any opinion polls saying a majority supported the idea. I expect a poll would have said the opposite. Putting together the ideological pressures from the left nationalists in the party, the frustration of dealing with the private producers who were challenging the taxes we levied, and the feeling that we in cabinet wanted to act and not just react to others' demands, we decided to proceed with legislation to bring the potash industry under public ownership. We introduced two pieces of legislation: the Potash Corporation of Saskatchewan Act, which gave legislative status to the crown corporation created earlier by order-in-council, and the Potash Development Act, which set out the provisions for acquisition by PCS of the private potash companies in Saskatchewan. The most startling feature of this act was the power it gave the government to expropriate, if necessary, the private potash holdings. We also wrote into the act the formula to use in determining compensation to be paid to any expropriated private owners. We didn't want the owners taking us to court, and some unfriendly judge awarding them a punitively large amount.

The debate that ensued was long and bitter. The potash producers, supported by local chambers of commerce, the opposition parties, and national right wing lobbies, mounted a massive media campaign against nationalization. One of the more clever ads made reference to an unsuccessful shoe factory the CCF had set up in the 1940s. The ad pictured two left shoes and asked mockingly, "Can a government that failed at the shoe business learn the potash business?" Fortunately, from our perspective, the Liberals and Tories never thought to ring the bells. The legislation passed, and we had the power by order-in-council to expropriate mines. Again we were fortunate. Some mine owners decided to negotiate with us and we were ultimately able to acquire as much of the industry as we wanted (40%) through negotiations. Industry spokesmen maintained, and to some extent they were right, that they negotiated with a gun to their heads.

Only after we acquired mines did we start polling. The results said that nationalization was not a popular issue: PCS was not popular, and nor was the government. In fact, in the fall of 1976, we were 15 percentage points behind the Conservatives led by a man, Dick Collver, who came from Alberta and had only recently settled in Saskatchewan. We had a fight on our hands! (In 1982 our polls lulled us into thinking we didn't have a fight, and we lost. One of the things I've learned is that it's better to know the bad news and know you've got to fight.) As a government we spent a lot of time on potash. Everybody knew we were in trouble, and so we went out and worked. The managers we put in to run PCS knew the NDP was in trouble and therefore their company was in trouble. They had to perform.

In addition to anything we did, we also got lucky in 1977 and 1978. We had no major labour problems, and the potash industry conveniently turned around from its brief slump in 1976. Rising potash prices brought us as much good luck as rising land prices brought us bad luck with the land bank. By 1978 our polls showed that a majority of Saskatchewan people, over 60%, approved PCS and the government's potash policy—largely, I would argue, because it was running smoothly and making money, not for any philosophical reasons, much as I'd like to think the Saskatchewan public is attuned to the left.

Conclusions

What do these two programs teach us about the potential for government? First, both were dramatic initiatives that served as cornerstones of government philosophy. They fit well with what most New Democrats thought an NDP government should be doing. The opposition parties also considered them dramatic programs that were **not** a cornerstone of their philosophy. They were ideal issues on which to clash. In both cases the government and the party were committed to persuading the public to our side. Both policies were legislated; both led to public ownership; both turned out to be within the constitutional capacity of the province, and both generated considerable, protracted and determined opposition from many sources.

These policies also raised the problem of government accountability to the people. In the public mind the only mechanism of

accountability was electoral censure. Traditional legislative accountability existed through the crown corporations committee and esti-
mates, but the public considered this as insufficient.

My central conclusion is that, regardless of the theoretical powers
of the state, realization of any lasting social or economic reform requires
as the most important factor long run public support. If ideology rides
rough-shod over the deeply held prejudices, beliefs and ideals of the
community, in the end the community will always win. Before you
proceed with a reform, you should believe that, at some time in the
future if not right away, you can obtain public support, or at least
acceptance, for what you are doing. In the case of potash we didn't have
public support when we started, but we hoped we could get it and we
did. In the case of the land bank we had public support when we
started—we were elected on the program—but when it was in place it
raised an idea, public land ownership, which is not acceptable to
Saskatchewan people.

Socialists need to learn two lessons. We know in general what kind
of society we want: a land of equal opportunity, generous income
redistribution from rich to poor, social justice, a world at peace. We
have failed, I believe, to present this global view of New Democrats in a
non-threatening way. Our vision doesn't have to be acceptable to
everybody, but it must not turn off over half the population. One
pollster has summarized our problem as follows: "When you ask the
question which party is least likely to represent your own interests, 61%
of people cite the NDP right off the top."[5] When you have 61% of the
people who won't even consider you as an option, it is hard to get into
power to implement reforms.

Here is the second lesson. Given a program within the limits of
public acceptance, our duty as New Democrats is to get out and
convince the public of the program's worth, and not take public support
for granted. Crudely put, politics is hard work and the art of the
possible.

I turn briefly to Leo Panitch and the social contract between
government and labour. I don't have as rigid a view of the subject as he
does. I haven't travelled through Europe and read books on it, but I
have considerable experience in Saskatchewan. I have negotiated with
public sector unions, and know the problems on both sides of the table.
For two reasons I conclude that the NDP, if intent on obtaining office,

needs to enter into a dialogue with the union movement about the content of future NDP government policy. First is the process of convincing the public that both of us—NDP and unions—will act responsibly when in power. After all there is a potential conflict of interest. The union movement is an integral part of the NDP, yet when in power a NDP cabinet will have to write labour legislation and bargain as employer with public sector unions. We have to convince people we won't sell the farm to the unions. Second, it is much easier to cope with problems if you have laid some ground rules ahead of time. That doesn't mean the NDP must specify, for example, a specific public sector wage guideline in the nature of the federal "6 and 5" program. But in the past we have, before getting elected, failed to admit even in principle the existence of inevitable real problems between the party and unions. Dialogue is useful, whether or not we draw up a formal "social contract" at the end of it.

In Saskatchewan at the moment there is a debate underway in both the NDP and union movement about the relationship between the two. One side within the NDP says we would be better off without the unions. Turn 'em loose. We have to fight with them when we get elected, so we may as well fight with them beforehand. That is not my view. I think the unions and NDP are natural allies. On the other hand, when the NDP again forms the government, there will again be differences of opinion between us and the unions. It is useful to search out accommodations ahead of time, or at least to agree, while we are out of office, on how we will resolve future problems.

---

[1]*New Deal for People: Program for Progress* (Regina: Saskatchewan NDP, 1971), p.1.

[2]*A New Direction: Saskatchewan Liberal Statement of Policy '75* (Regina: Saskatchewan Liberal Association, 1975), pp. 1,2.

[3]*New Deal for People*, p. 8.

[4]Ibid., p. 6.

[5]Allan Gregg (of Decima Research), quoted in Toronto *Globe & Mail*, 28 February 1983.

Discussion

Session One

Peter Warrian: Elwood, I'm not a politician. I'm a trade unionist but I fully understand that both politics and collective bargaining are the art of the possible. You talked about the Saskatchewan experience, and limitations on the land bank policy and the potash takeover. In pursuing those two programs you were up against the limits of the possible. Yet in both cases, we actually get to Leo's questions: that is, we're also up against the limits of our political culture, of people's attitudes towards government, people's attitudes on the family, on property ownership, etc. You're both on different tracks but are running into each other and you come to a profound issue for all of us. The real question is how can we extend those limits, **extend the range of what is possible**, both in our policies and in the mobilization of people. If we only operate within the current status quo, we'll never get anywhere. None of us is happy with the current situation; we want to change the distribution of economic and political power, but we must also extend the limits of what is possible. And that is a problem equally for the party and unions.

As well, Elwood, you discussed the appropriate role of the trade unions within the NDP. None of us have worked out, even in an ideal sense, what the role of trade unions would be in a socialist economy. We don't have any good answers on that.

Certainly the NDP and unions would not be better off without each other. Trade unionists have learned in many bitter struggles in the 1980s that we are up against the limits of government economic policy. The good times in the resource boom following the Second World War won't happen again. No longer can unionists make an easy split—pursue collective bargaining at work and support the NDP at election time secure that, whatever party wins, collective bargaining can proceed as usual. Even in the NDP we've tended to split labour policy from economic policy and frankly that can't go on.

On the matter of a social contract between labour and a NDP government, I would say, labour and the NDP can't live without each other, but sometimes we can't seem to live with each other! Every NDP government we have known has got into a rumble with the trade unions, particularly with public sector unions. Canadian experience is not unique. Look at the current example of tension between French unions and a socialist government committed to a policy of restraint.

Art Kube: I lived in Austria for many years, and that's where I had my cultural upbringing. It is worth understanding that the Austrian workers' movement controls a large part of the country's economic pie, and with that control they can get things done. Social democrats must understand they can't have political power unless they also have economic power. Social democratic parties should try to strike agreements with labour on an incomes policy—provided the savings in wages make the workers equity owners. Creating worker-owned capital, administered by the union movement, is what the Swedes are trying to do. It's an area where Canadian social democrats have an important role. Unless workers obtain that sort of stake in the economy, I think talk of a social contract is a hell of a lot of window dressing.

Allan Blakeney: I want to address first some of the comments made by Leo Panitch, and his conclusion that social contracts are a failure in western Europe. I was puzzled by that. Obviously they are a failure measured against their authors' objectives, and I'm sure every other social policy is as well. But that's not relevant. The only thing that is relevant is whether they're a failure measured against the alternatives, because that is all we have to choose from. We cannot choose between a policy and an ideal. We can only choose between a policy and another policy. And they are both going to be down here in the grubby world.

One objective of these social contracts, as you said, was a voluntary promise to restrain wages to allow the government to reflate the economy without generating inflation. And I ask, did they fail? Did they fail compared with North America? Were their inflation rates higher, and their unemployment rates higher? I'm puzzled if you say they are a failure. I think every one of those countries that had a "failed" social contract had a lower unemployment rate and a lower inflation rate. Therefore, compared with the alternatives, I say they are a success. I don't mind if the policy doesn't achieve all of the objectives painted for it. If it moves us forward, if it deals with unemployment and inflation, then I count it a success. You say the policies have effectively restrained wages, and their chief effect is the restraining of wages of lower income people. And I say, perhaps so. You know facts that I don't. But in order to convince me that it is a failure, you have to tell me they were restrained more than they were in North America where we practise capitalist collective bargaining in a tough economic situation. Do poorer workers fare better in Austria or in Alberta? There may indeed be a third choice. If you are saying that social democratic social contracts are now passé in Western Europe, and there is something better to look forward to, fine. But it is not an effective argument to say that these social contracts failed because they failed to achieve all their proponents' objectives. I don't regard that as an argument against any government's social policy.

I want to make another quite different comment on your argument, Leo, about the need to build a social movement. We do need a melding of politics and culture. For that we need cultural and political and social institutions—not only governmental institutions, but non-governmental as well. With that we can heartily agree. I'm sure all of us grit our teeth every time we look at television and see it pulling people out of our environment, where we could build some sort of a cultural milieu, and taking them to Dallas or wherever. We have been putting altogether too much reliance on elected social democratic parties in office. They are the elected arm of the progressive movement. When in office, they can do not a bad job. But they are, particularly when in office, a rather ineffective educational arm. The NDP outside the legislature, and sometimes even when out of office, has not done a particularly effective job as an educational arm. If I may say so, I don't think the trade union movement has done a great job of proselytizing its members any more than the NDP has done. The co-operative movement is almost dead from the point of view of proselytizing for a more progressive society. I didn't think I'd live to see the day when the cutting edge of progressive thinking would come from the Catholic bishops, but that's where it is—not only in terms of expressing progressive ideas, but of proselytizing with them. If you want to hear people talking about progressive ideas and how to reshape society, don't bother going to a NDP or union meeting, go down to a Catholic parish meeting. That tells us something about the job that needs to be done.

It's easier of course to state the problem than to propose the cure. We have all been hammered by so many gods that have failed that we are a little jaded. I am not as sanguine as some who believe that all we need do is set up structures whereby people can participate. We have to do more than that. I see high participation organizations which don't grab me, if I may put it that way. Where I live, probably the highest participation organizations are the pro-life and pro-choice groups dealing with the abortion issue. Lots and lots of people are interested in that cause. It is not only a matter of participation, but a matter of reinvigorating progressive roots which have become seared by failure or partial success.

Tom Gunton: Two brief points. One for Elwood. I was a bit surprised that the examples you used were from your first and second terms of office, not your last. Could you address why you think you lost the 1982 provincial election, and to what extent the loss is related to a lack of accountability of your government. In hindsight can you suggest ways in which you might have prevented that defeat? For Leo I would like to reiterate Allan Blakeney's point. It's really a question of what works best among a number of bad alternatives. Nothing works particularly well!

Grant Notley: Leo, I don't want you to get away with the notion that a social contract, at least as we envisaged it when writing the *June 22nd Statement*, was just a wage control policy. Second, I agree with Allan and Tom that we should measure western European performance relative to Canada, not on the basis of some ideal. I listened with interest to your critique of European social contracts, but I don't believe anyone who has visited Scandinavia could argue for a moment that Canada is a more egalitarian society—not even Saskatchewan or Manitoba with their experience of NDP governments.

You would be great, Leo, as an opposition politician. Ray Martin and I could use your philosophical evaluation of what the Tory bastards are doing in this province. But we really have to define socialism in clearer ways than your brief comments on price controls and nationalizing the banks. We can't with intellectual honesty make sweeping generalizations—at least not when you are a practising politician faced, as Elwood was, with the real limitations of political power.

Jim Russell: I'd like to bring things down to the grubby world. As an unsuccessful NDP candidate in this Tory paradise, I'll start by agreeing with Allan Blakeney's comments about what's practical. I want also to stress the importance of images and impressions. My own experience, from running as a candidate in Edmonton, is that the NDP's association with the trade union movement is both extremely important to the public image of us, and not very helpful. That is a blunt reality. At one level, as a New Democrat, I am sympathetic to the trade union movement and its concerns, and think we share an enormous amount. But when we get on the doorstep in active election campaigning, we suffer from two problems. One is that people see us as selling the farm, for practically nothing, to the trade union movement. That may not be true, but the perception hurts us badly. The other problem is that we are not supported by the unions effectively during election campaigns in this province when the going gets tough. It's important that the NDP and unions either work together, or not pretend to do so.

Elwood Cowley: I'll start with the question I liked best: why did the Saskatchewan NDP lose the 1982 provincial election. I have been through that now 842 times—early in the morning and late at night. The simple answer is that we obviously lost touch with what people were thinking and got beaned by a very effective Tory campaign. You asked, Tom, why I talked about programs from our first two terms, not our last. Part of our problem may have been that in the third term we built on what we had started before. We were spending our time making sure that the potash corporation worked, defending our uranium policy, and trying to keep the land bank going. We didn't do a lot of new things. Also, to some extent we ran out of ideas on the social side. Some NDP members perceive us—whether true or not—as having spent too much time on economic development and not enough worrying about the sick, the lame and the poor.

Come the election we missed underlying concerns of the public about the economy and what they were getting out of it. The Conservative program contained essentially two policies: elimination of the provincial gasoline tax (which appealed to everybody's desire to be like Albertans and have cowboy boots and a stetson) and reduced mortgage rates, a more fundamental issue. Elimination of the gasoline tax offered people economic relief out of the revenue we were putting into a heritage fund. At the time many homeowners were facing 20% mortgages. The Conservatives promised 12 1/4% fixed interest for the first $50,000 of a mortgage, and that was damned attractive to people facing a near doubling in mortgage payments and unsure how to pay them. We were also lulled into a sense of false well-being by our poll results. We got the right answers to the questions we asked, but we didn't ask the right questions. The Conservative policies responded to the concerns our questions didn't pick up.

How could we have won? Had we introduced a similar mortgage program to the Tory's and some kind of direct return to the public of a portion of provincial resource revenues, we might have changed the results. However there are a million people in Saskatchewan and a million different ideas on why the NDP lost.

I want to turn to Art Kube's statement that you can't have social power unless you have economic power. We were very conscious of that in the government, and we were trying via the crown corporations to get our hands on the economic levers accessible to us. Is the union movement conscious of that idea? It has always surprised me, for example, that Canadian unions have never, in my experience, put much effort into controlling their pension funds. I've never seen a strike over control of a pension fund or decisions made in investing it. Pension funds contain a tremendous amount of potential economic power for the union movement, and they have never effectively exploited it. That says one of two things: either there is no support from union members to gain control, which may indeed be the case; or, like many of the rest of us, union members are unsure what to do with the money if they did control it, and it's easier to stay put.

That returns us to the dialogue that needs to take place between the NDP and trade union movement. Are we going to maintain a purely adversarial system of bargaining between future NDP governments and unions representing public sector workers, and then a week before the election union leaders say to their members the NDP are the good guys to vote for? It doesn't work. I'm not being critical of the unions. Adversarial collective bargaining is the system we currently have. We can't change it overnight, but in the long run we have to modify it.

We need a level of trust. My experience in direct labour relations is limited, but I was the minister responsible for two unionized crown agencies: the Potash Corporation whose workers were represented by the Steelworkers and Energy & Chemical Workers unions; and the Liquor Board, whose workers were represented by the public sector union, Saskatchewan Government Employees Union. The differences between the two were like night and day. I didn't negotiate directly with the potash unions, but I knew, when I got a call from one of their representatives, that there was a problem I should address—not a wage demand. The problem might be, we are being told "this", we don't think messages are getting through, is "this" really the position of the government or the board of directors, can you clarify things with the managers? That worked well; there was a high level of trust. With the Liquor Board, on the other hand, the Government Employees Union wanted to bring in three professional bargainers, catch me drunk at night and negotiate with me by myself, hoping I'd sign a contract knowing nothing about it. I'm not a professional bargainer, and I wanted professional help on my side. Frankly, there wasn't trust on either side. We need to develop a higher level of trust prior to elections. You can call it a social contract if you want.

My last point is to ask, what is the general idea that the NDP is pursuing? As I recall the 1950s and 1960s, the NDP had a vision—primarily to improve the welfare state. The raison d'être of the CCF was to create a society where health care would be universally accessible, and you'd be able to go to good schools—hospitalization, medicare, education, good roads, clean water, that sort of thing. Everybody could agree on them. Below that the party had specific programs aimed at realizing the goal. The great majority of people identified with this vision. They might not agree with the nitty-gritty of CCF programs and hence vote Liberal, but they weren't frightened by the CCF vision. Our vision now has somehow either narrowed or vanished. The worst thing that could happen to us as a party is to end up a collection of single-issue groups, none of which agree with any other. We don't have an umbrella to attract people to us; we need again a clear vision.

Leo Panitch: What criteria do we use to measure a social contract or government policy? It's not clear we can measure it as Allan Blakeney suggested. I resent the implication that it is nice for egghead academics to measure policy against ideals but in the practical world it is policy against policy. On the contrary, I find that politicians are full of illusions about their power and only discover, to their cost, the limits of their power once in office. There are a number of possible explanations why the rate of inflation is lower and rate of economic growth higher in Sweden or

Austria relative to Canada and the United States, reasons apart
from the nature of any social contract. Historically these countries
are different. Austria and Sweden are more equitable societies
because they have strong, deep and long socialist traditions. Also
there are extensive price controls in the Austrian case and a massive
manpower planning program in Sweden. For reasons dating to
Nazism and the Second World War, there is substantial public
ownership of Austrian industry and banks. Finally, socialist parties
are stronger in Sweden and Austria than here.

To say in Canada, let's set up this framework where labour and
capital equally manage the workplace, where government en-
courages workers to organize collectively and where all parties are
committed to full employment and better public accountability,
well, it's naive. Since there is no strong mass socialist movement
in Canada, you are walking into an arrangement where you lack
the strength to back up your demands.

We should also be clear that the international capitalist recession
has come to Austria and Sweden, as elsewhere. Advocates of a
new social contract are *often* not honest about that. I will give you a
disturbing example. At a conference, involving the CLC and the
Catholic bishops, CLC president, Dennis McDermott, said West
Germans live in a civilized society that would not permit the
Canadian unemployment rate. His research staff did not feed
him accurate information. The West German unemployment
rate in the spring of 1984 exceeded 9%, not far below ours.

With regards to the Catholic bishops, I strongly agree with their
position. It is both disturbing and exciting what they are doing. I
was at a labour rally sponsored by the Ottawa District Labour
Council on May Day. Bishop De Roo from Victoria addressed it.
He and other bishops were distributing a new pamphlet issued on
May Day. It was very good. Unlike advocates of a new social
contract who stress a partnership between labour and capital,
their pamphlet stressed the priority of labour, historically a fundamental socialist theme. The left is talking about a social partnership while the bishops are talking about the priority of labour.

I entirely agree with Allan Blakeney about the uncertainties of participation. People can participate on hospital boards and close off abortion possibilities in the hospital. If we are democrats, we can't be afraid of that. We have to mobilize to fight it out. We can't avoid it—not that you were suggesting we avoid it, Allan. We have to teach skills. The CCF and the union movement in the 1930s taught skills, participatory skills, how to debate, how to argue in socialist terms. We have lost much of that. It is a serious loss.

I'll end with a comment on people upset that I insist the social contract is about an incomes policy. Obviously, it's not just an incomes policy. I stressed that people enter into the social contract with the best of intentions, expecting it will be more. But it is largely about reassuring business that we can resort to Keynesian stimulus and still retain business confidence. When you play the game of seeking business confidence, businessmen up the ante and when you try to control their incomes, by price controls for example, they say, oh no, we won't invest under those conditions. You're left with wage restraint.

Session Two: Labour

Unions in an Information Economy

Arthur Kube

I am speaking here not as president of the British Columbia Federation of Labour but as an individual who faces the same dilemma many of you are facing—namely, in what direction should socialism be moving in this country, and how can it address the future?

If I had addressed that topic just ten years ago, I likely would have talked in the context of an expanding industrial society. It was a period of fast economic growth and increases in real disposable income for working people. I would have assumed that "my kid is going to have it better" and that the inequities of the system would be wiped out by enlarging the economic pie. For most of us in the trade union movement it was a relatively simple world. It was "them against us", and with the exception of the odd economic downturn, we were winning. We had our dreams and a good number came to fruition.

If I had addressed that topic around 1980, I would have talked in the context of a post-industrial society. By then uncertainty had replaced optimism. In North America economic growth was slower. Energy prices and hard-core unemployment were rising, while real wages were not. But all was not bleak: the public sector was continuing to grow; community groups were fighting for social entitlements; Canadians were generally accepting a multicultural society. I would have finished by talking about current economic problems as an aberration, to be blamed on scapegoats such as the OPEC cartel and foreign competition. Provided we adopted certain corrective policies, economic performance would return to what we had thought in the 1960s as normal. The union value of "them against us" was, however, no longer as clear; we faced complex problems. I would have noted that the simple slogans of the right were appealing to a disturbingly large number of people.

Arrival of the "information society"

Today we are in a period of great transition. Not only in the labour movement but in the whole society, we are searching for answers. Part of the labour movement thinks we are still living in an industrial society, but in fact we are entering the "information society". Some of us are struggling to seek answers to the problems of this transition. I am certain of one and only one thing: we can never revert to the industrial society we knew in which there were enough jobs to create full employment. The sooner we overcome that illusion, the sooner we can concentrate our energy on making the transition to an information society less painful and more conducive to human development.

Technological change, which has ushered in the information society, undeniably increases the wealth of our society but it also eliminates jobs. Frequently the lost jobs are union jobs, in industries where workers had previously successfully organized to redistribute wealth with some measure of equity. Industrial economies are as wealthy as before, but we are producing and distributing wealth in a manner that guarantees major structural problems.

I always operate on some very simple assumptions. The first is: as long as a nation can meet its international obligations, the economic problem is really a process of redistribution.

The arrival of an information economy means that an increasing proportion of society's wealth is in the form of human potential, and not physical assets. Wealth as physical assets means technology and the machinery embodying it. Wealth as human potential is intangible because it is synonymous with human skills, education, creativity and culture.

No longer is the gross national product a good measure of a country's wealth. Let me give a few examples. If you smash up your car and have it fixed or purchase a new car, then you contribute to the GNP. Had you driven safely, you would not have contributed to the GNP. We can solve our energy problem by increasing the supply of very expensive oil from the tarsands. For each barrel of oil produced this way we increase the gross national product by the world price of oil. Alternatively we can solve our energy problem by investing in conservation. Conserving one barrel of oil may create as many (or more) jobs as producing one, but if it is cheaper to conserve than supply, it will result in a lower measured GNP. Yet in the broad sense of wealth, it is the second solution that creates more wealth. While it lowers GNP, it increases human potential to solve problems without relying on running down the natural resources of our planet.

We must turn away from the GNP as measure of the nation's wealth. It does not measure the health, physical and mental, of a people; nor does it measure the extent of literacy. Yet both health and the ability to communicate by reading are basic criteria by which to measure a nation's real wealth.

Let me also dispense with two buzzwords, "productivity" and "international competitiveness", both inspired by an undue respect for maximizing GNP. Every day they are being sounded like a clarion call in this country. It is implied that, unless we are extremely productive and able to compete in international markets, our chances for high incomes and a meaningful life are small. Assume, for a moment, that we play the productivity/competitive game. We could increase labour productivity (output per worker) by massive capital investments in new machinery. We could improve our competitive position relative to newly industrialized countries, such as South Korea and Taiwan, by lowering our wages towards theirs. What would be the result? We would actually have less employment, and those working would become the working poor. But that is not necessarily the end of the game. The business and political elite of these Asian countries might then force down further the wages of their workers, in order to restore their competitive edge. If you play it out, you will find it to be a no-win game for working people, both here and overseas.

The American economist, Lester Thurow, is correct in arguing that our economy is organized into winners and losers, that it resembles a "zero-sum game":

> Our economic problems are solvable. For most of our problems there are several solutions. But all these solutions have the characteristic that someone must suffer large economic losses. No one wants to volunteer for this role, and we have a political process that is incapable of forcing anyone to shoulder this burden....
>
> Our political and economic structure simply isn't able to cope with an economy that has a substantial zero-sum element. A zero-sum game is any game where the losses exactly equal the winnings. All sporting events are zero-sum games. For every winner there is a loser, and winners can only exist if losers exist....
>
> When there are large losses to be allocated, any economic decision has a large zero-sum element. The economic gains may exceed the economic losses, but the losses are so large as to negate a very substantial fraction of the gains. What is more important, the gains and losses are not allocated

to the same individuals or groups. On average, society may be better off, but this average hides a large number of people who are much better off and large numbers of people who are much worse off. If you are among those who are worse off, the fact that someone else's income has risen by more than your income has fallen is of little comfort....

The problem with zero-sum games is that the essence of problem solving is loss allocation. But this is precisely what our political process is least capable of handling.[1]

Investment in new machinery embodying new technology may enhance the wealth of the firm's shareholders and those workers with the skills to operate the new machinery, but it may impoverish the workers who worked the old machinery with "old" skills. Even if the sum of benefits of the winners exceeds the sum of costs to the losers, that is scarce comfort if you happen to be among the losers. In the past, when our economy was regularly growing at 5% or more per year, it was easier to compensate the losers. But now output per person working is stagnant, and the distribution problem is more acute.

Let me address another trend of the 1980s: "downsizing government". Over this century, as industrial employment grew and industrial workers bargained for better wages, their demand for public services also grew. The result: a major extention of the public sector. We on the left tended to take for granted universal social services supplied by a large public sector. We were impatient to get on to other battles. But recently powerful groups on the right have mounted an effective campaign against so-called "big government". This counter-attack has won the support of a disconcertingly large number of people, including many who ultimately stand to lose from "downsizing". Why have so many people supported a conservative position? They have supported it largely, I think, because government bureaucracies have become desensitized to the users of public services. The politicians who presided, in North America, over the introduction of welfare state programs had, by and large, little commitment to the underlying philosophy of a community sharing. They introduced the programs grudgingly, as political expediency to keep office. How could we expect such politicians to be sensitive to the users of these programs? Could we expect them to agree, for example, to users participating in decision-making over the provision of these services? Hardly!

The power brokers in our society are over fifty years in age. This age group in general, and the power brokers among them in particular, are wedded to the beclouded values of the protestant work ethic. The writer Paul Hawken[2] has an appropriate image. While there are always resourceful human beings bearing up under economic difficulties and adapting to new circumstances, above them are the would-be "practical men" who are, in effect, slaves, as Keynes said, to the ideas of some defunct scribbler. For these "practical men" the activities that contribute to society are essentially only those directed to the production of goods and accumulation of capital. They are prepared to reward workers who manufacture armaments, for example, more generously than those who provide child care services. They think it appropriate that society reward far more generously those who accumulate financial capital than those who further our culture. As long as values such as these predominate among Canadians, it will be extremely hard to realize structural change. It is therefore incumbent that socialists challenge these acquisitive values, and promote values that genuinely contribute to society. Without such values people will never create the political will necessary to make structural change.

Let me sum up this part of my argument. I challenge the use of GNP as a true measure of a nation's wealth. I challenge the notion that we can solve our economic problems by seeking to increase our competitive international edge. I challenge the emphasis on producing "things" over "services". I challenge the values of power brokers in this, and many other, capitalist countries.

What's to be done?
Challenging what is without offering any solutions does not contribute much to the debate. First, I do not ignore the value of maximizing industrial production, if achieved with due respect for all the external costs. We should increase the volume of wood fibre cut—and simultaneously devote more money to reforestation. We should increase in the long run the size of our fish catch—and preserve spawning streams and build up fish stocks. We should invest in pollution technologies. But even then we shall not achieve full employment as presently defined: everybody who wants work able to work 40 hours or more per week.

We must examine work redistribution. In my mind there is no question the time has come for a reduced work week, or a reduced work year, or a reduced work life. Ultimately that is the only way to deal effectively with technological change. Is our demand for goods so insatiable that, however productive our economy becomes, we shall always want more? Does a point never come when we take some of the fruits of increased productivity in the form of shortening what constitutes "full time" work? In the 19th century workers campaigned to get rid of the twelve-hour day, and after that, the ten-hour day, and finally established the eight-hour day as the norm. For several generations we have believed in the eight-hour day, but it is not sacred.

While reduced working hours must ultimately prevail, a creative response to the information society suggests other means to create work. To take advantage of new technology a society must be prepared to increase its investment in human development: in education and on-the-job training. With more time devoted to training or educational leave, firms need more workers to maintain output levels, and training institutions need more staff.

We must make a new commitment to equality in society. One important area is taxation. Not since the Carter Commission of the 1960s have our politicians said anything substantial on this subject. (Postscript, 1985: In the 1984 federal election the NDP raised the issue, and forced the Liberals and Conservatives to promise tax reform, but the new Conservative government has yet to do anything.) Special interest groups have lobbied for countless tax concessions. Whatever the rationale for adopting them, these concessions have primarily favoured those with power and wealth. High *marginal* income tax rates for the rich are a nuisance, but skilled accountants can juggle their income so that they wind up paying *average* rates no higher than working people. Progressive income tax in practice is not working. The best way to tax the rich is by initiating more serious taxation on consumption: progressively oriented "value added" taxes that levy higher rates on industries producing luxury goods. A commitment to equitable taxation is not as easy as it sounds. It is not simply a question of making millionaires pay. As I look at people in attendance at this conference, I suspect that over half of you are "rich" in the statistical sense of earning well above the average for working Canadians. An equitable tax system means that you too may well have to pay more.

If we want to change Canada, we cannot leave the doors and windows of our economic house wide open to every gust, every storm that comes along. I am not proposing to batten the openings to the point that all becomes stale inside, but we must be prepared to some degree to protect ourselves from international economic fluctuations. We should examine the feasibility of exchange controls, as an alternative to the Bank of Canada's attempts to keep hot money in Canada by making our interest rates follow the erratic swings in American rates. Today, the holders of the huge sums in "eurocurrencies", currencies of one country owned by citizens of another and exempt from national controls, can undermine economic planning in any one country by speculating against its currency. Such was the fate of the French franc when Mitterrand assumed power in 1981. To preserve stability of its exchange rate, the besieged country must adopt unreasonably high interest rates that hurt its domestic economy.

In international trade I make the case for "fair" commodity price agreements. Too often, international trade between third world exporters of primary commodities and first world exporters of manufactured goods has been unfairly biased. Too much competition among the first group depresses primary prices relative to manufactured good prices. Major exporting nations of particular primary commodities should bargain with importing nations to determine prices that allow a fair return to those who work to produce them. Many in the industrialized countries may resent paying higher commodity prices, but this is a reform that can realistically increase the wealth of the world's poor, and reduce the international paranoia that politicians and defence contractors exploit to justify spending $800 billion annually on armaments.

I am a feminist. One aspect of our undervaluing those performing services, as opposed to making things, is our undervaluation of women. In most cultures most child rearing is performed by women. Feminists are persuading men to assume a larger share, but still the imbalance persists. Therefore, when we in Canada pay child care workers low wages and afford low status to those raising children at home, we are primarily penalizing women. In Scandinavian countries child care workers earn a decent wage, because these societies value their services. Ultimately what is at issue here is that we be prepared to pay a fair "social wage" to all who are productive, both in and out of the marketplace. A civilized society does not structure its economy to encourage winners at the expense of losers; it structures its economy to meet people's needs in terms of opportunity, equity, and the chance for a fulfilling lifestyle.

As socialists our options for the next decade are few. Either we build a social consensus and community harmony on our capacity to redistribute wealth, or we shall have a society in which social brutality prevails. The British Columbia Social Credit government is an example of what happens when socialists fail to win popular support. The weak and dependent, the "losers", became the principal target of official government policy.

There are many issues about which I have not talked. In conclusion I mention one, decentralization. Traditionally socialists have been excessively centralist, comfortable with macro-level planning by central governments. We are hopefully learning the fundamental truth that people can more effectively participate at the micro-level. Adapting our politics to this truth will be difficult.

I have raised many questions and offered, perhaps, a few answers.

---

[1] L.C. Thurow, *The Zero-Sum Society: Distribution and the Possibilities for Economic Change* (New York: Penguin Books, 1981), pp. 11-12.

[2] P. Hawken, *The Next Economy* (New York: Holt, Rinehart & Winston, 1983).

The Case for a New Social Contract

John Richards

British trade unionism, it seems to me, has erred in conceiving labour and capital as both permanent forces, which were to be brought to some equality of strength by the organization of labour. This seems to me too modest an ideal. The ideal which I should wish to substitute involves the conquest of democracy and self-government in the economic sphere as in the political sphere, and the total abolition of the power now wielded by the capitalist. The man who works on a railway ought to have a voice in the government of the railway, just as much as the man who works in a state has a right to a voice in the management of his state. The concentration of business initiative in the hands of the employers is a great evil, and robs the employees of their legitimate share of interest in the larger problems of their trade.

Pitfalls of Socialism
Bertrand Russell

I   Industrial Relations: A Social Contract in Trouble

I have divided this essay in three. In this, the introduction, I outline some of the troubles surrounding the present social contract defining relations between organized labour and capital. By far the major part is the second, which makes the case for labour participation in management. The argument in this part is somewhat technical. Bear with me; the economic distinctions are useful. The final part defends the principle of "incomes policies"—political mechanisms to limit some prices, wages in particular sectors, and other incomes.

What is a Social Contract?

From Thomas Hobbes on the right to Jean-Jacques Rousseau on the left the core idea of those who have conceived of the state as a social contract is that individuals and groups contract, implicitly or explicitly, for mutual gain in the political marketplace, just as in the economic marketplace. The idea of the state as executor of a social contract can be a conservative rationale for the status quo. To summarize Hobbes: however unequal the distribution of income and power under the 17th

century English monarchy, those at the bottom in some sense acquiesced to the monarch's authority; the alternative was an anarchic
society in which they would enjoy even less. Simultaneously the idea
can be radical because it implies the exercise of state power is illegiti-
mate unless it arises from some form of contracting among organized
groups—classes, regions, races—within society.

Whether used as metaphor or as description of an explicit deal
among interest groups, the term "social contract" conveniently em-
phasizes the simple truth that groups and individuals do bargain over
the statutory and administrative rules that in turn provide the framework for exchange in both economic and political markets.

Take an important example. A bitter 1866 strike in the Sheffield
metal trades was catalyst for a decade of political haggling to negotiate a
new social contract for British industrial relations. During the first
century of the industrial revolution, British judges viewed trade unions
as an infringement upon the rights afforded to employers and employees as individuals under the common law—itself a kind of social
contract amended over the centuries—to enter voluntarily into labour
contracts. Over time an increasing proportion of workers concluded
that individual contracting in accordance with the common law was
fundamentally unacceptable. In the course of this particular strike the
union hired agents who blew up the cottage of a "blackleg" (i.e.
"scab") worker.

Initially, bourgeois spokesmen responded with calls for anti-union
legislation to end what they declaimed as the "Sheffield outrages". On the
other side attempts to rally support for the union movement culminated in
the formation two years later of the Trades Union Congress as a confederation of British trade unions. By Disraeli's Reform Act of 1867, large
numbers of (male) workers were able for the first time to vote. This
restrained the conservative impulse to "solve" the problem by anti-union
legislation. The contemporary British leaders, Disraeli and Gladstone,
were in a way arbitrators in a union-management grievance, competing to
be engaged by the principals. Over the ten years each won and lost voter
endorsement, and each had a hand in drafting new legislation that gave
unions a secure legal status and certain legal rights to limit employer access
to non-union labour. Following strikes during 1872 in Montreal, Hamilton
and Toronto calling for the nine-hour day, John A. MacDonald passed
legislation that in all essentials copied emerging British law.

Senator Wagner and his aides performed a similar role when, sixty years later in 1935, they drafted and guided through the United States Congress the National Labour Relations Act (better known as the Wagner Act). Wagner considered his Act a social contract necessary to resolve the bitter social conflicts then raging over union recognition in basic industries. Canadian workers lobbied for similar Canadian legislation, and in the 1940s the federal and provincial governments enacted versions of the Wagner Act. When the CCF was elected in Saskatchewan in 1944, for example, labour lawyers associated with the party drafted a model statute, giving that province the most "pro-labour" legislation of any North American jurisdiction. With modifications the Wagner Act has served as the basis for the social contract governing labour-management relations in Canada as well as the United States for the last half century.

The principles of the Wagner Act—some drawn from precedent, others newly conceived by the Act's authors—have become every bit as "self-evident" to North American labour leaders as Thomas Jefferson's Declaration of Independence was to the American revolutionaries. The Act proclaimed the right of workers "to bargain collectively through representatives of their own choosing". It established a powerful administrative tribunal, the National Labour Relations Board, to administer the Act. It introduced the concept of "unfair labour practices", effective constraints against employer interference in the formation of unions. It established a set of "certification" rules whereby a particular union could obtain a legal monopoly on the exercise of the collective bargaining function for a group of workers, and another set of rules for "decertification".

Collective bargaining under attack

Unlike the Declaration of Independence, however, the social contract embodied in the Wagner Act is losing legitimacy, even among union members. Symptoms of declining legitimacy abound. In the United States unionized workers as a proportion of the nonagricultural labour force declined from a third, as recently as 1960, to under a fifth today. This trend has not yet hit Canada, where unionized workers have remained a stable proportion (between 36% and 40%) for the last decade.

A second symptom is the chorus of (neo)conservatives arguing that governments have made it too easy for unions to obtain certification and too hard for dissatisfied workers to decertify a union, and that the rules surrounding strikes are too lenient (e.g. secondary picketing should be restricted, some or all public sector strikes should be banned). The ultimate goal for many of these critics is "right to work" legislation that restores freedom of contract as the basis for the social contract between worker and employer. In Canada this remains a minority sentiment for the moment, but can we Canadians successfully resist ideological currents that have become prominent in both Britain and the United States? My province, British Columbia, is obviously among the most polarized jurisdictions in North America on this subject. Powerful trade unions face a conservative government many of whose members talk in precisely these terms.

A third symptom is Canada's increasing rate of strike activity. In terms of working days lost to strikes per worker, Canada's ranking among major OECD countries has worsened, and during the 1970s was second to Italy's. As a percentage of time worked, average annual strike activity more than trebled between the period 1960-64 and 1977-81. We must avoid conservative hysteria on this issue. Unionization of the Canadian labour force increased over the last two decades. Therefore the number of collective agreements and the potential for strikes also increased. In most years time lost to strikes remains less than one half of one percent of time worked. While Canada's strike activity has increased, it has also increased—if not as much—in other OECD countries. The rise is, however, a symptom of increasing frustration between workers and employers.

A fourth symptom are public opinion surveys. They provide uncertain results, but the widespread stated lack of confidence in union leaders by Canadians—and the results among union members and NDP supporters are not much more positive—is ominous in the long run for the labour movement, and the left in general. (See the survey on this subject in Chapter X.)

One effect of the 1982 depression was to shift the prime economic concern of Canadians from inflation (how to control it, how to obtain personal wage/salary increases) to unemployment (how to reduce it, how to create jobs, how to assure personal job security). In terms of the questions posed in Table 1 this has been a shift from an area of perceived strength to perceived weakness in union performance. Again the difference in responses between the average Canadian and union member is not large.

Table One
Assessment of Trade Union Performance in Specific Areas

Many people say that unions have different responsibilities. I'm going to read a list of some of these responsibilities and I'd like you to tell me, for each one, what kind of a job you think unions are doing. Would you say unions are doing an excellent, good, only fair or a poor job in doing everything they can to...

		Canadian average	Union member average
		(percentage responding excellent and good*)	
1	get higher salaries for their members?	68%	66%
2	get more fringe benefits such as longer vacations and greater pension coverage for their members?	67	66
3	ensure that their members have a safer and more enjoyable work environment?	57	58
4	ensure job security for their members?	50	54
5	ensure that their members have greater access to job training programs?	39	40
6	ensure the economic survival of companies?	19	27
7	co-operate with governments and private industry to plan the economic future of the country?	20	24

* *Respondents' options were the above four element range plus "no opinion". Percentages were calculated from total sample responses, including "no opinion".*

Source: The Decima Quarterly Report (Toronto: Decima Research Ltd.), III 4 (Winter 1982).

The final symptom is the public perception that collective bargaining as practised in Canada exacerbates inflation and reduces employment. In the survey discussed in Chapter X, nearly two thirds of the sample agreed with the statement, "Union demands often contribute to unemployment". While the proportion of non-unionized workers agreeing exceeded that for the unionized, nonetheless by a small majority the latter also agreed. The current (1985) Canadian inflation rate is low relative to the recent past. Unemployment and productivity growth are presently more important public issues of debate. But industrial countries have achieved price stability only by generating economic depression and massive unemployment.

Two ingredients for a new social contract
    At the risk of simplifying a complex subject, I think two ingredients need to be added to any new industrial relations social contract: acceptance of the legitimacy of labour participation in management, and of government intervention—especially at times of serious inflation—to control certain wages and other incomes.
    Let me start with the idea of government intervention to control incomes. Incomes policies have taken many forms in different countries, ranging from the Swedish example of highly centralized tripartite bargaining among leaders of government, labour and business, to direct government control as in the case of the Canadian Anti-Inflation Board from 1975-78. Some examples have been "good", others "bad". I do not want to discuss here any administrative details except to suggest that, in a country as profoundly decentralized as is Canada, a successful incomes policy would probably have to be administered through provincial governments. In the discussion that follows, others will doubtless present the arguments against incomes policies. Here I want simply to state the basic tactical and strategic arguments in favour.
    An organic link between the trade union movement and a social democratic political party can enrich both, and here in Canada it should be maintained. But trade unions are a special interest group that, like any other, pursue public policy designed to redistribute income towards their members and away from the rest of society. Tactically, an incomes policy addresses the widespread public mistrust that the NDP, a party in formal alliance with the trade union movement, will "give away the farm to the unions". Support for an incomes policy is an effective symbol to the large group of mistrustful citizens that the NDP is able to define policy independently of the union movement. This group, we must realize, comprises many potential supporters—among non-unionized and even unionized workers. Stra-

tegically, a carefully constructed incomes policy can improve the trade-off between inflation and unemployment. There are legitimate reasons for the overwhelming public demand that politicians "do something" about high inflation when it occurs, and the policy choice is effectively between some form of incomes policy and serious deflation of the economy. Deflationary policies wreak an abhorrent cost in terms of unemployment. Imposition, under any circumstances, of an incomes policy is a contentious idea on the left, and is opposed by a majority of trade union leaders. I do not want to dodge the debate, and have made what I hope is a convincing case in Part III.

The idea of a new social contract will entail some substitution of political bargaining for collective bargaining. In exchange for some restriction on the scope for collective bargaining, labour must receive an enhanced role in corporate management. That is the second new ingredient. Significantly, in those countries where some form of incomes policy has been accepted by labour, labour enjoys more power over corporate management than typically exists in North America.

Canadian socialists need to transform "democracy in the workplace" from a utopian slogan into a central political demand—and ultimately into a central component of industrial relations practice. Political parties need utopian ideals; they also need feasible reforms to serve as link between present reality and future goal. The appropriate reform in this case is, I want to argue, "codetermination"—the right of workers in large firms to elect as members of their respective boards of directors a number equal to that elected by shareholders.

Much of what is meant by "left" in politics is the belief that ordinary people can achieve major goals via collective action—in political parties, in co-operatives, in unions and other institutions. Much of what is meant by "right" is scepticism about the potential for collective action, and a counterbelief that the role of the state is to set rules (for example those defining private property) that permit individuals to pursue individual goals. While I disagree with much of Panitch's conclusions on policy, I agree that western industrial society is undergoing a neoconservative reaction to the deficiencies of the Keynesian/welfare-state social contract. At best it is a half-truth to describe this social contract as a product of the left, but given these attacks many on the left feel obliged to defend it unequivocally. That is self-defeating. Parts of the conservative critique are accurate, in particular its attack on the deficiencies of large public bureaucracies. We on the left legitimately retort, what about the excesses of concentrated, unaccountable owners of corporate capital? but two sins do not make a right. The traditional socialist cure of central planning and nationalizing the "commanding heights" is, to many, worse than the disease of corporate power. The first argument for codetermination is simply that it addresses the problem of unaccountable power exercised by corporate management without directly increasing the role of the state.

For socialists, however, the prime reason to support codetermination is to advance democracy at work, a fundamental domain of most peoples' lives. One of the unambiguous results of the survey reported elsewhere in this volume (in Chapter X) is the desire by workers to exercise more influence over decisions at work than they currently do. But let us not ignore two other arguments. A social contract involving codetermination will probably be more economically efficient than one involving collective bargaining alone. And, relative to collective bargaining, labour participation in management enables workers to bargain over certain issues more effectively with the representatives of financial owners.

One statistic that suggests the importance of this reform is the difference between the average rate of growth of labour productivity (GNP per employed person) in countries that rely on collective bargaining alone and the rate in countries that have introduced labour participation. Canada, Britain and the United States are the three major industrial countries that rely on decentralized collective bargaining as the primary component of their respective industrial relations systems. West Germany, Austria, Denmark, Netherlands, Norway and Sweden are the six western European countries with the most developed forms of labour participation in management. During the 1970s the average annual rate of labour productivity growth was approximately 1.2% in the first group, 1.9% in the second group. Of course, these statistics are only suggestive. Many other factors in addition to industrial relations determine rates of productivity growth.

II Labour Participation in Management

Analogous to the rise of political democracy, industrial democracy has become central to labour relations in the economic marketplace. Industrial democracy is unfortunately an expression of frustrating imprecision. We shall use it to cover all arrangements (including but not restricted to collective bargaining) whereby production—as distinct from managerial—workers exercise a significant measure of control within their respective firms. A few introductory distinctions are in order.

The problem of size

For many economic activities large scale organization and its corollary, division of labour, are, by many orders of magnitude, more efficient than small. (This does not deny that beyond some limit larger firms become less efficient.) The larger the scale, however, the more people are involved, and the more decisions that must be made. Beyond some low threshold of scale the cost of *direct democracy*, of direct participation by all personnel in the making of all decisions, becomes prohibitively costly in terms of the time needed to assemble a coalition sufficiently large to adopt any particular option, and to monitor one another's compliance.

One alternative is *contracting out*. Technical economies of scale are realized, but smaller functionally related groups form themselves into separate firms maintaining legal separation. Co-ordination is realized by means of detailed contracts stipulating the services and payments among the interrelated firms. Here we face a different problem. The more interrelated the firms, in the sense that each is necessary to the economic well-being of the others, the more tempting is it for one or more firms to exploit the remainder by holding out in contract negotiation.

Another means to realize the efficiencies of large scale organization is to create a distinction among the personnel within a firm between the "bosses" and "workers". The bosses are invested with *managerial rights*, the authority to co-ordinate and—within a range of prescribed options—to give orders to the workers, who agree to obey in exchange for payment. Much of the meaning of capitalism is that managerial rights are exercised by those who supply finance. But in principle they can be exercised by those who supply labour, or by a third party. In turn, much of the meaning of private property under capitalism is not the right to buy and sell physical assets, but the right to buy and sell the right to manage, either directly as an owner-manager or indirectly via appointed agents. Under capitalism the right to manage others is for sale.[1]

Two forms of industrial democracy

For most economists this state of affairs is perfectly satisfactory provided competition exists in the relevant markets: for the firms' output, for the hire of workers, and for the relevant property rights. For the left this state of affairs has never been satisfactory. We have always argued that workers want, and have the right, to exercise a major control over the affairs of their respective firms. This right can take essentially two forms, or some combination thereof: detailed *contracts* (collective bargaining agreements) negotiated by representatives of those who supply labour and those who supply finance, or direct *participation in exercise of the managerial function.*[2]

Level, Scope and Degree of Labour Participation

A first distinction to be made is the *level* at which worker authority is exercised. At the lowest level workers may participate, usually directly, in making shop floor decisions affecting the organization of work. In North America, most discussion has turned around the introduction of greater worker autonomy at this level (e.g. the "quality of work life" trend). At the highest level workers participate indirectly by electing representatives to the firm's board of directors. Intermediate level participation can also exist (e.g. joint labour-management committees at a plant level).

The *degree* of industrial democracy over any specific management function may range from non-existent, in the case of a unilateral exercise of authority by the owners, to absolute in the case of "worker control"—by which I mean elimination of the shareholder's or the state's management right over private or nationalized firms respectively. The degree of worker control need not be all or nothing; it may be intermediate.

A third distinction is the *scope* of industrial democracy. Are all management decisions subject to industrial democracy, or only those in particular domains? For example, during the 1970s, the health and safety policy of firms became in certain provinces, most notably Saskatchewan and Quebec, a matter to be decided in labour-management committees composed of equal numbers of workers and managers. Provincial statute required firms to establish these committees.[3]

Why organize?

The argument for labour participation in management requires that we distinguish clearly between two reasons workers seek to combine for mutual support. The first is the "relative numbers" problem: there are many fewer capitalists than workers. The second is the problem of "human capital": much of the capital required for any firm's operation is in the form of workers' skills, skills moreover that are specific to the requirements of the particular firm.

1) The relative numbers problem

One consequence of the numerical imbalance is the unequal impact of arbitrary decisions by one party on the other. For any one worker arbitrarily to withdraw his labour will usually have a minor impact on the financial well-being of his employer. Conversely an arbitrary employer's decision to withdraw employment is a major factor in the financial status of the workers affected. Workers, if organized, can erect mechanisms (grievance procedures) that raise the costs to employers of arbitrary behaviour.

A second consequence arises because the cost of organizing to exercise a measure of monopoly power in a market rises with the numbers involved. In the absence of a concerted effort by workers to organize, the degree of competition among workers offering their services will almost inevitably be far more intense than among employers seeking to hire. When one side of the labour market can effectively organize and the other cannot, the outcome will likely be less desirable (in terms of a lower level of employment and output) than under conditions of countervailing power where both sides organize.

2) Industry- or firm-specific human capital

Human capital is an idea conceived, obviously, through analogy with physical capital.[4] Investment in physical capital entails costs in terms of foregone consumption: the workers engaged to create a capital good cannot for the duration produce consumer goods. Once in place the capital good contributes benefits in terms of an increase in the level of productivity of workers using it. Investment in the improvement of a worker's mental and manual capacity is entirely analogous. When, for example, a secretary takes a leave of absence to take a course in word processing, he/she is generating costs in terms of the memos untyped plus a prorated share of the costs of the college offering the course. The benefits of this investment in human capital arise from the secretary's increased productivity after training.

We must next distinguish between *general human capital*, which can be expected to raise a worker's productivity in many industries, and *firm-* or *industry-specific capital* whose productive potential is restricted to the worker's present firm or industry. Examples of the former are the investment in elementary education skills of literacy and numeracy, or of an engineer's investment in learning computer programming. Examples of the latter could include a farmer's learning the operation, maintenance and repair of a combine harvester, or a file clerk's learning the details of a particular company's filing system. The financial analogue is investment in a machine with multiple uses, or in a specific-purpose machine the return from which depends entirely on the success of the relevant venture.

The more general the human capital the more likely the costs of its acquisition will be borne by the worker himself or, in the case of general education, by the taxpayer. If the employer pays for the acquisition of general human capital, he will be concerned about his ability to reap the benefits. He may, for example, require the worker to reimburse him if he quits prior to the passage of a specified period of time. Enforcement of such contracts is difficult. In a non-slave society ownership of human capital, once created, obviously cannot be exchanged, nor can it be repossessed if someone other than the worker paid for it. Accordingly the worker whose skills have been enhanced will typically pay for his training, either directly or in his capacity as taxpayer funding education.

In the case of firm-specific human capital the employer may be willing to pay for its acquisition since, by definition, the benefits can only be realized within the firm. Here the concern about who reaps the benefits is on the side of the worker. To maintain the worker in his employ, the employer must pay at least as much as the worker's best alternative. But outside the firm the worker's investment in human capital is unproductive, and the wage he can command may be correspondingly low. However if the employer attempts to capture all the benefits, then the trained worker has no incentive to work more productively than the untrained. Training improves a worker's *potential* productivity; his *actual* productivity depends on his effort and that of co-workers.

We have presented general and specific human capital as distinct. It is more accurate to think in terms of a mix of the two. In practice the cost of human capital acquisition is frequently shared between employers and workers. An employer may pay trainee-employees a salary, but below that which they could earn in alternative unskilled jobs.

To the extent labour is unskilled or possesses general human capital only, the employer can consider all workers of comparable training to be perfect substitutes as employees. Similarly workers can be confident of their ability to command equivalent wages in alternative employment to those offered by their present employer. Workers may well organize because of the relative numbers problem, but not because of their collective human capital.

However, one broad generalization we can make about the evolution of industrial society is the rise of the relative importance of human to physical capital and, with increasing labour force specialization, of specific to general human capital. The combination of uncertainty, complexity and specific human capital places skilled workers in a situation analogous to those who finance specific-use plant and equipment. Workers and suppliers of finance have a common interest in maximizing the return on their respective investments and, obviously, a conflict of interest in its distribution.

Both workers and "financiers" need to organize to protect their long run interests. Workers with scarce skills in short supply (e.g. bright young computer engineers) can negotiate individually with employers to protect their human capital. For most workers collective organization has advantages. Economies of scale in negotiating provide cost savings to workers if they collectively designate an agent to negotiate standard contracts for them. Collective organization can create sanctions against employers who might be tempted to renege on prior contracts when market conditions offer the potential to hire for less.

Managing vs. *Contracting*

We mentioned earlier that worker organization to exercise industrial democracy will be a combination of essentially two forms. It is time to consider these forms more closely:

1) Direct worker participation in exercise of the managerial function

Workers can strive to exercise all, or some part of, the managerial right, the residual right to do with a firm's assets and employees anything not forbidden by law or constrained by contractual obligations. Worker exercise of management can be either direct or indirect and, as we discussed earlier, it does not eliminate the unpleasant necessity that, to some extent, an hierarchical relationship must exist between manager and worker if the efficiencies of large scale organization are to be realized. Worker participation in management makes feasible, however, less authoritative managerial styles.

2) Detailed contracting (collective bargaining)

Alternatively, workers can opt for a system in which their agents (the union) negotiate with the agents of suppliers of finance (the management) agreements specifying the distribution of costs and benefits, rights and obligations. Implicit in such contracts is that the residual rights be exercised by management, who are ultimately accountable only to the financial owners.

Collective bargaining is the form that labour organization has assumed in Canada. Why change it?

The first reason is to advance democracy; the second is to advance overall efficiency in the economy. The efficiency argument turns essentially on how well different industrial relations systems permit workers to capture benefits from their investment in human capital. By contrast, the relative numbers problem is simpler; at its core is conflict over distribution of corporate revenue between profits and wages. Where the relation between parties is primarily adversarial, it is preferable to write an explicit contract (collective bargaining agreement) specifying the rights and obligations of each. Joint decision-making may well end in stalemate. The human capital problem is more complex. Suppliers of finance and of human capital have shared as well as conflicting interests. Both parties need to collaborate to maximize the total return to their combined investment, even though they are in conflict over its division. The parties must consider costs and benefits over long periods of time, and are subject to uncertainty about future outcomes. As anybody who has tried knows, writing detailed contracts is cumbersome when the contract must cover a long period during which many things may change, and change in unpredictable ways.

There have been attempts within collective bargaining to provide incentives for workers to realize their potential productivity, and for employers to share with workers the benefits of specific human capital. Wage scales that rise with work experience and training are one such arrangement. Productivity-related payment schemes are another. Skilled workers agree to train apprentices if the collective agreement guarantees seniority. Workers agree to their own retraining if guaranteed preservation of income and seniority rights. These arrangements are less than perfect. For instance, rarely do wage scales have enough steps to reflect skill gradations.

Consider briefly the problems associated with productivity-related payment mechanisms. They can assume many forms: simple piece rates for individual workers, productivity bonuses among a team of workers where productivity is joint and cannot be attributed to any individual worker, combinations of fixed wages and profit sharing among a firm's entire work force. Worker desire to maintain equity among incomes will legitimately limit the use of productivity-related systems.

Still, if making reward more directly related to productivity increases average worker productivity and incomes, workers might well desire to make some trade-off between equity and productivity-related payment. Further, productivity-related payments also enable a firm to absorb shifts in demand for its output by changes in average labour costs, rather than changes in size of its labour force. That means workers can choose—unpleasant as the choice is—between fewer jobs at higher wages or more jobs at lower wages. Except for simple piece rates, however, all productivity-related mechanisms depend on financial data supplied by management. Where workers have no control over management, as is the case under collective bargaining, they mistrust the data's accuracy and tend to oppose such mechanisms as devices for management to cheat.

In answer to the question, why change industrial relations? let us be Talmudic and ask another. Why do those who supply money as opposed to labour want to exercise management? In any capitalist economy those who supply finance have available a panoply of financial instruments far larger than that available to workers. Admittedly much finance is supplied on a "contract" basis equivalent to collective bargaining. Firms enter into contracts with banks for access to credit; they sell fixed-interest bonds. However firms also issue common shares which, while offering only a residual claim on corporate income, are unique in that they permit suppliers of finance to purchase a share of ownership, the essence of which is the management right.

Put simply, major investors in a firm do not buy debt instruments alone; they want equity. To write detailed contracts, in a context of complexity and uncertainty, is more costly than to hire agents (managers) to represent their interests. The advantages of ownership are the ability to make decisions quickly, avoidance of the costs of contracting in advance, and lowered costs of gathering information.

Exercise by those who supply money of the management right is obviously a central feature of a capitalist economy, as economists as diverse as Karl Marx and Milton Friedman have insisted. Its extension to organized groups of workers on a large scale is a radical change! The advantages of a share in management to capitalists, the supplier of finance, are the same advantages that workers, the suppliers of human capital, wish to enjoy. We might summarize them as follows:

1) Lower cost of gathering information

For any given level of effort the management of a firm can usually generate better information about its financial prospects than can an outside agency. Legislation may require firms to publish prospectuses and financial reports for the benefit of financial investors, and to provide certain financial information to a union certified to represent its employees. Despite such requirements, "inside information" remains valuable.

Learning what the other side knows is frequently an expensive activity under collective bargaining. To secure a low wage settlement, management may bias its statements of future revenues and costs, and union negotiators mistrust management-supplied financial data and forecasts. In the interest of increasing the settlement, union negotiators may exaggerate the willingness of workers to undertake collective action, and management negotiators accordingly discount such claims. Even if the bargaining dynamic is stable and statements by each side converge towards "truth", the time and resources expended can be large.

2) Flexibility of decisions

Several factors render management decisions more flexible than those constrained by collective bargaining. First is the freedom from precedent. One reason the Wagner Act created a new administrative tribunal to adjudicate labour relations conflicts was to free such decisions from the weight of past judicial precedent. But labour relations boards in different jurisdictions have, over time, built up their own body of precedent that becomes embodied in collective bargaining agreements. This new body of precedent may provide useful rules for conflict resolution; it also limits exploration of efficient alternatives. A second factor is that a management decision can be revised at any time, whereas collective bargaining contracts typically can be revised only when the contract is up for renegotiation. Costs are lower for management-made than for contractual decisions, but are not zero. To avoid such costs management will not review its decisions continuously, but the ability to revise at any time is important. Third, being subject to easier review, management decisions can be more ad hoc than contractual decisions. Management can afford to experiment with novel decisions not all of whose implicatons have been thought through. If large unforeseen costs arise, revision can be made relatively quickly.

Admittedly, for many contexts contracting is clearly preferable to managing, and labour participation in management will never remove the need for workers to negotiate collective bargaining agreements. We can summarize the *disadvantages* of managing in the following two problems:

1) Exercise of control over agents

How can "owners", using the term to cover shareholders and workers, simultaneously delegate authority to their agents and yet prevent them from pursuing their own interests which may well diverge from those of the owners? Debate has swirled around this question since, in the 1930s, Berle, Means and Burnham introduced the "managerial revolution" thesis. Proponents of the thesis argue that corporate managers have, as companies become more complex and share ownership more diffused, effectively usurped the ability to control from shareholders. Critics of the thesis emphasize the constraint from the capital market if managers deviate far from profit maximization, presumably the shareholders' goal. If managers do not maximize profits, the price of shares will drop and a new set of owners may take over the firm, replace the management with one that does maximize profits, and realize a capital gain. The takeover threat provides a constraint on manager behaviour, but it leaves a wide range of managerial discretion, and hence the shareholders' problem.

Labour participation in management would involve worker representatives in more complex decisions than those posed by collective bargaining. Hence workers, like financial owners, might find it more difficult to control their representatives. However the problem already exists in the context of collective bargaining. Rank-and-file union members delegate responsibility to professional union staff to act as agents in bargaining and grievance procedures, and I doubt labour participation in management would render accountability significantly more difficult.

2) Stalemate in the decision-making body

To require parties, whose interests are antagonistic, to participate in joint decision-making may produce polarization and stalemate. When bitterness between spouses in a failed marriage reaches a critical level, no decisions can be made jointly. If they must nonetheless make decisions about matters affecting them both, child custody for example, they may need an explicit contract and legal sanction to enforce compliance. To the extent industrial relations systems are rules to manage conflict, the failed marriage analogy is relevant. But, as I have argued all along, the relationship between workers and suppliers of finance cannot be described as purely adversarial.

The Case for Parity

We have to this point argued that *some* worker participation in management is preferable to reliance on collective bargaining alone. But how much? Should workers be content with minority representation on boards of directors, or should they aim for "workers' control", the elimination of all managerial authority exercised by suppliers of finance, or something in between? Before attempting an answer, consider three complex labour relations issues where board level worker participation has, in other countries, proved important: development of shop floor participation (e.g. "quality circles"), introducton of major technological change requiring new skills, and worker desire for stability of earnings.

Repeated industrial psychology studies have concluded that, within broad limits, workers prefer a participatory, non-authoritarian managerial style in their immediate place of work, and that such styles actually improve productivity. And, as the survey in this volume shows (Richards & Mauser), workers want more influence over decisions at the point of work ("personal decisions") than over those at higher levels of management. None of this makes superfluous the matter of worker participation on boards of directors. A persistent obstacle to expansion of "shop floor" democracy has been worker suspicion that any such experiments constitute management attempts to manipulate: to weaken worker commitment to collective bargaining through the union, to increase productivity without corresponding increased worker benefits. Successful experiments in "shop floor" democracy have usually required elaborate preliminary planning between union and management, and creation of joint union-management committees to supervise the experiment. In effect labour participation in management at higher levels has proved necessary for its success at the "shop floor". In terms of our previous discussion, such labour-management committees lower the cost to workers of gathering information and monitoring the other side.

Turn to technological change. Assume a firm has the option of undertaking a major investment in plant and equipment embodying new technology, and the sum of benefits unambiguously exceeds the sum of costs. Assume further the project requires not only the replacement of old physical capital by new, but of old human capital by new. When collective bargaining is the sole mechanism whereby workers and shareholders can contract, the union response may be to exercise a veto because contracting to capture benefits for and avoid costs borne by workers is too difficult. If workers participate in the management decisions surrounding the project, they are better placed to assess the project's impact and net benefits, and to obtain compensation, by retraining to other positions within the firm or by generous severance for workers whose skills are rendered obsolete.

Undoubtedly codetermination in the German iron and steel industry since World War II is significant in explaining the faster labour productivity growth in German relative to French and British steel-making. Most of the technological change has been labour-saving. German workers were in a better position to force shareholders to share with them the gains from improved technology than their counterparts in France and Britain, who relied to a large extent on militant trade union bargaining to resist technological change and consequent employment decline.

These two examples, particularly the latter, illustrate the problems that face labour as a minority on the board of directors. Management decisions to realize major projects entail complex trade-offs, and if worker representatives are to take joint responsibility with the financial owners for decisions that entail current costs in exchange for a share in future expected benefits, they legitimately want to assure they are not outvoted when it comes time to allocate the benefits. Thus, unless workers have at least parity, it is doubtful they will accept any major substitution of participation in management for contracting via collective bargaining.

Our third example introduces the problems that arise if workers attempt to assume total exercise of the management right, i.e. to eliminate shareholder equity altogether. Imagine an economy where workers alone exercise the managerial function. Financiers would now be in a position analogous to workers in a capitalist economy and, like them, would in general refuse to supply finance in exchange for a share in net income. Why should they, any more than workers in a capitalist economy, trust the other side's definition of net income? Better to opt for a contractually prespecified rate of return. The implication of workers' control is that labour's claim to corporate income be residual, the income left after paying all other claims, including a fixed charge for finance. Labour income is here directly related to firm productivity.

The closest approximation to such an economy is Yugoslavia's. The country's constitution embodies the principle of workers' control, and the state-owned banking institutions typically supply finance subject to contractually fixed rates of interest. An important disadvantage to workers is that they are now forced to bear all the risk of uncertainty of their firms. Given the overwhelming importance of employment income to the financial well-being of the ordinary worker, he may well prefer to share exercise of the management right with some capitalists, in order that he can induce them to supply some finance in exchange for a share of residual income and a corresponding share of the risk. By spreading the risk, the worker can more readily arrange to receive at least part of his income in the form of a fixed wage.

We have illustrated the problems of workers participating in a board of directors on a minority basis, and of workers exercising a monopoly of the managerial function. My conclusion is that, ideally, both workers and suppliers of finance share the managerial right in such a way that neither can be outvoted. That implies parity. For Canadian socialists the most relevant brief for parity in codetermination is Bullock's Committee of Inquiry on Industrial Democracy, established by the last British Labour government during the 1970s.

In 1974 the Labour Party came to power. At the time, leaders of the Trades Union Congress (TUC) and the Labour Party were jointly committed to the thesis that a radical extension of labour participation in management was a required reform: to increase democracy in an important domain and, by improving labour relations, to improve the capacity of British industry to innovate and increase productivity.

Support for industrial democracy was never unanimous within the TUC and Labour Party, and was opposed by business lobbies. The business representatives on the government inquiry (chaired by Lord Bullock) issued a dissenting minority report in which they accepted a measure of labour participation, but opposed parity. Since publication of the inquiry's report in 1977 British politics have become bitterly polarized. Members of the Conservative government, elected in 1979, have been completely disinterested in such proposals. The Labour Party has been weakened by its internal debates on Marxist themes. For many on the left of the Labour Party, Bullock's recommendations were suspect for their overtones of "class collaboration"; for many on the right of the party they entailed too much conflict with financial interests. In Britain, at present, only the Alliance (Liberal—Social Democratic Party) favours unambiguously the principle of codetermination.

Among European trade unionists prepared to support codetermination it is worth emphasizing that parity has been the expressed goal. To quote Bullock:

> We believe there must be a joint approach to decision-making in companies, based on equal representation of employees and shareholders on the board. In our view it is no longer acceptable for companies to be run on the basis that in the last resort the shareholders' view must by right always prevail. There must in the future be a new legitimacy for the exercise of the management function within a policy framework agreed jointly by the representatives of capital and labour. We believe that this new legitimacy is essential for the long-term efficiency and profitability of the private sector and for the ultimate success of the economy itself.

> We do not think that this will be achieved unless employee representatives are fully involved in, and committed to the work of the board, and share equally with the shareholder representatives the responsibility for the board's decisions. In our view it is unreasonable to expect employee representatives to accept equal responsibility, unless, through equal representation on the board, they are able to have equal influence on the decision-making process. In West Germany this was an important argument leading to the extension of employee representation from one third to 50 per cent, which was effected in 1976....

> We believe that the main benefits of representation at board level in terms of improved industrial relations and greater efficiency will result from the greater acceptability to employees and trade unions of board

decisions in which employee representatives have been fully included and for which they have taken equal responsibility. In our view these benefits may never be realised if employees are not equally represented on the board: first, because a minority group of employee representatives will be less willing to become involved in the formulation of policy, if at the end of the process they know they can always be overruled by the shareholder majority; second, because the credibility of employee representatives in the eyes of their constituents will be reduced, if those constituents conclude from the proportions on the board, that their representatives are powerless. This view is confirmed by the West German experience of parity and minority systems, evaluated by the Biedenkopf Commission in 1970. Comparing experience of parity representation in the coal, iron and steel industries with that of minority employee representation in other parts of German industry, the Biedenkopf Commission reported that there was more commitment and co-operation at board level, where employees were equally represented ...[5]

Bullock discusses many problems posed by such a reform: confidentiality of corporate information, minimum size of firm (2000 employees) to which board-level parity should apply, a triggering mechanism to assure workers want board level participation (majority support among a firm's employees in an election called on the subject, one third minimum required turnout), the relationship between collective bargaining and worker participation in management. Much of this discussion is specific to Britain, but his "2X + Y" parity formula has excited sufficient debate to warrant mention. X is the number of directors apppointed by the firm's shareholders; the same number is to be elected by workers; Y is a smaller group to be co-opted with the agreement of each of the other two groups.

III   Incomes Policies: An Unpleasant Necessity

As I stated at the beginning, the argument *for* incomes policies is simple. They improve the trade-off between unemployment and inflation. By all means the left should emphasize the disadvantages of incomes policies (and seek to minimize them), but it is hypocrisy not to admit that alternative policies to control inflation entail worse disadvantages—serious deflation of the economy and high unemployment.

A good point of departure is 1974. That year marked the beginning in Canada of two significant events: double-digit inflation and stagnant aggregate productivity per person employed. Both inflation and productivity statistics are summaries of complicated social relations, and economists continue to disagree about the appropriate explanations, despite having constructed models of increasing elegance. Where uncertainty exists, ideology prevails, and some will doubtless want to make such a charge against the following.[6]

Some on the left argue that inflation is a minor annoyance, and we should not expend energy on devising policies for price stability, particularly when inflation rates are low (compared to the recent past) and unemployment high. However unemployment and inflation are inextricably linked, and to be credible we on the left must address the link. The widespread public demand to contain inflation does have a reasonable basis. Inflation does not produce the same proportionate change in all wages and prices. Some change more than others, and thereby some are randomly enriched at the expense of others. Inflation also diverts entrepreneurial energies from the production of "real output" to the generation of information about price changes, and hence generation of speculative income. Speculative demand in turn exacerbates relative price movements. An obvious example is volatile housing prices arising from speculation in real estate in recent years.

Given the failure in many countries of conventional Keynesian fiscal/monetary policies to contain inflation during the 1970s, intellectual and public support grew for an economic mutant, monetarism, which had survived for decades as a minor species at the University of Chicago and a few other niches. Monetarists argued that inflation could only occur if "validated" by accommodating governments providing an ever-increasing money supply. If government applied a well-publicized rule for a low fixed rate of growth of the money supply, organized groups would quickly learn that inflation was to be contained, would lower their inflationary expectations, and lower their demands for nominal wage and price increases.

Monetarists have linked a "quantity theory of money" explanation of inflation to a vigorous critique of government intervention intended to regulate the aggregate level of economic activity. Keynesian policies of fiscal stimulus have, it is argued, a short term effect of raising employment at the current wage and price levels. But the additional demand must inevitably raise some prices. Workers realize their real wages are declining and demand higher nominal wages, which in turn reduce aggregate demand for labour. Ultimately a new equilibrium arises, at a higher inflation level, but with no change in employment. For monetarists the unambiguous cause of inflation is excessive government demand on economic resources; the prescription, an end to activist intervention by government.

While union spokesmen have, for obvious reasons, resisted the monetarists' conservative policy implications, some have been attracted to this side of the inflation debate because it attributes no role to organized labour in explaining inflation. The monetarists conclude that, like any monopoly, unions distort relative prices, but they do not affect the rate of change of prices.

The alternative line of analysis of inflation, which has been labelled "post-Keynesian", attributes a central role to "vested interests", including large corporations, professional associations and trade unions, that have segmented the market. Where "vested interests" are important, *real* prices/wages (allowing for inflation) change slowly due to the complexities of recontracting among the strong interest groups involved. Only in markets where buyers and sellers remain unorganized can changes in market forces of supply and demand produce rapid change in real as well as nominal prices.

An inevitable by-product of legislation to encourage collective bargaining is to deny employer access to non-union labour, to increase segmentation in labour markets, and thereby weaken the effect of changes in market forces on wage rates within unionized sectors. The result is some ability for unions to set wage rates in terms of "fair shares" as perceived by their members: "fair shares" relative to past rates of growth of real wages, relative to wages in other regions and industries, or relative to corporate profits. Unions are certainly not alone among interest groups in utilizing their market power to set the prices of their respective services in terms of self-defined "fair shares". Corporations price to realize target rates of return; in a similar manner professional associations set fee schedules, and agricultural marketing boards set prices.

How do "vested interests" define respective "fair shares" and how do they affect inflation? An interest group's "fair share" is the summary consensus among members of the group of what constitutes the optimal strategy for maximizing the group's long run income. The senior executives of a major corporation may decide that a 20% after tax rate of return is the maximum obtainable without serious competition from other firms, and adopt a "fair" pricing strategy that marks up costs to realize that goal. For many years the United Auto Workers defined a 3% annual growth of real wages as their "fair share". "Vested interests" involving many individuals cannot quickly redefine their optimum strategy when external events change.

For many reasons the sum of "fair shares" during the 1970s exceeded the available national income and serious inflation ensued. Why in the 1970s and not the 1950s or 1960s? One reason is that North American economies during the last decade experienced a dramatic decline of average annual labour productivity growth. Compared with an average annual rate of 3.5% between 1951 and 1973, Canadian labour productivity (output per person hour in the non-farm business sector) grew between 1974 and 1981 at an average rate of 0.7%, i.e. virtually not at all. Since 1973 any increase in income by one group in the labour force has essentially been at the expense of some other. For example, dramatic rises in the relative prices of key commodities (oil, cereals) enriched some Canadians, but obviously at the expense of others. Given their definition of appropriate "fair shares", organized interest groups that faced income declines responded by raising their nominal prices and wages to restore their "fair shares". That in turn triggered a wage-price spiral. The policy prescription that follows is imposition, when necessary, of some form of incomes policy—some political mechanism to limit wages in particular sectors, other incomes, and some prices.

To summarize the two positions, academic economists, politicians, central bankers, businessmen and trade union leaders, have advocated inflation policy based on the relative importance each attaches, on the one hand, to growth in the money supply caused by excessive government spending and, on the other, to "vested interests" launching wage-price spirals. To be crude, public policy to control inflation must comprise some combination of controls on money supply and direct incomes policy. Monetarists have emphasized the former, advocates of a "social contract" the latter.

In the late 1970s monetarists won the policy debate in a number of countries—including Canada, United Kingdom, and United States—and have since conducted experiments designed to demonstrate the efficacy of their solution. They succeeded in restricting the supply of credit, but initially the fundamental wage-price spiral persisted. The demand for money to finance economic transactions at higher price levels drove real interest rates to record high levels, collapsed ultimately the demand in interest-sensitive sectors, and produced a dramatic world-wide depression. Only after massive unemployment of men and machines weakened the price-setting power of large corporations and unions has inflation slowed. Monetarist policies, by lowering the available GNP to allocate, have themselves exacerbated the competition over income shares and contributed to potential future inflation if and when unemployment falls.

The alternative of an incomes policy is also subject to criticism. Any incomes policy implies some inefficiencies: more bureaucracy and further blunting of the (already very blunt) market processes whereby resources move from low to high productivity sectors in response to relative price changes. These costs are far less, I am convinced, than those entailed by vigorous government-induced deflation, which can leave people and machinery unemployed for years.

Because incomes policies interfere with collective bargaining, a majority of Canadian union leaders have consistently opposed them. Their reasons have been both good and bad. The good reason is that, too often, conservative governments have introduced incomes policies as a means to subtract from workers' collective power and to check wage income only. The bad reason is that union leaders have refused to address the external cost, in the form of inflation, from unfettered collective bargaining. So long as union leaders oppose in principle all forms of explicit income planning, and constrain the NDP to do likewise, they increase the probability that Canadians support monetarism, the most arbitrary form of incomes policy: restricting the supply of credit and public expenditures until unemployment is high enough to halt any wage-price spiral.

Whether organized as a semi-voluntary agreement among representatives of organized labour, business and government, or as formal government regulation (e.g. the 1975-78 Anti-Inflation Board), an incomes policy entails some centralization relative to the present collective bargaining system—in other words some subtraction from the freedom of individual unions to bargain collectively. Centralization is an undeniable disadvantage of all incomes policies. Their only virtue is that the alternative of *no* incomes policy has even worse disadvantages.

IV   Conclusion

Introduction of codetermination in major firms may be the appropriate quid pro quo if organized workers are to accept in principle the constraints on collective bargaining entailed by any incomes policy. That organized workers become "entrepreneurs" is the intelligent response to the current concern about productivity. The answer to the present problems of industrial relations is not "union bashing"; it is to adopt an industrial relations social contract that makes it easier for workers to make efficient decisions.

In part industrial relations change by evolutionary selection in which changes randomly arise, but survive only if they offer mutual advantage. But as we discussed at the beginning, social conflicts have often produced major changes in the social contract in a relatively brief period. The obvious question to pose is, are present difficulties sufficiently acute to permit further radical change? Inertia imposed by vested interests is clearly formidable. Corporate managers oppose labour participation in management for obvious reasons. The careers of union leaders, labour lawyers, arbitrators, mediators, etc. depend to some extent on the demand for the "output" of the present industrial relations system. If codetermination and incomes policies lower the demand for that output, the value of their specific human capital falls. It is unrealistic to expect the champions of change to come from that quarter. In a fundamental sense these are political matters.

---

[1]For a fuller discussion of these ideas see, for example, O.E. Williamson et al., "Understanding the Employment Relation: the Analysis of Idiosyncratic Exchange," *Bell Journal of Economics*, VI 1 (Spring 1975), pp. 250-78.

[2]I owe much of my thinking on this distinction to H. Landier, *Demain, Quels Syndicats? Essai sur la Crise du Syndicalisme en France* (Paris: Librairie Generale Francaise, 1981).

[3]For further discussion of these ideas see K. Newton, *The Theory and Practice of Industrial Democracy: A Canadian Perspective*, Discussion Paper 94 (Ottawa: Economic Council of Canada, 1977).

[4]The originator of the term "human capital" is Gary Becker. See his

classic work: G.S. Becker, *Human Capital: a Theoretical and Empirical Analysis, with Special Reference to Education*, 2nd. ed. (New York: National Bureau of Economic Research, 1975).

[5]*Report of the Committee of Inquiry on Industrial Democracy*, chaired by Lord Bullock, Cmnd. 6706 (London: HMSO, 1977), pp. 95-96.

[6]While this discussion draws from many sources, I want to admit at least some of the intellectual debts: C.L. Barber & J.C.P. McCallum, *Controlling Inflation: Learning from Experience in Canada, Europe and Japan* (Ottawa: Canadian Institute of Economic Policy, 1982); J.E. Meade, *Wage-Fixing* (London: George Allen & Unwin, 1982); M.C. Olson, *The Rise and Decline of Nations: Economic Growth, Stagflation, and Social Rigidities* (New Haven: Yale University Press, 1982).

Discussion

Session Two

Peter Warrian: John Richards stated it well when he defined the essence of a social contract as the relationship between labour and capital. For us at this seminar, the question is the appropriate role of the NDP in that relationship.

As a trade unionist I disagree with some of John's proposals, but I agree with much of his analysis. I agree that in a broad sense a social contract existed in Canada based on the welfare state and the Wagner Act. It lasted from 1945 to 1975. Our sense in the labour movement is that this social contract has been breached. We have been told that by employers and by neoconservative political spokesmen. What is going on in North America at the moment is more profound than declining union membership, stagnant productivity, and anti-labour poll results. A profound restructuring of the social contract is taking place.

With all due respect to John's presentation, we are not really here to talk about economic policies for the NDP. We can work those through over time. Why we are really here is to talk about politics and, more particularly, the relationship between trade unions and the NDP.

First, there is an alienation felt by some party activists towards the trade union movement—both in Ontario and in the West. Some people in the party just don't like trade unions. They think the party connection with labour is an electoral liability. But things are tough all over. As someone who works the other side of the street, let me say that many union activists are critical of NDP politicians who don't deliver, who resolve strikes by back-to-work legislation. As a professional trade unionist the party connection gives me more hassles than benefits on a day-to-day basis.

Second, the party cannot win without labour but conversely collective bargaining cannot deliver the goods for workers without the support of government policy, including many of the Wagner Act provisions that John referred to.

Third, there is a very serious problem in the relationship between public sector unions and the NDP when it is in power as government and employer. I don't have any magical solutions to this problem. Its solution requires a great deal of time, imagination, and patience.

Fourth, we are here trying to work out the relationship between the party in the West and in Ontario. In part it means working out the relations between labour and non-labour elements of the party; in part it means working out the relations between different provincial sections of the party with different regional interests.

Sam Gindin: While I think Peter Warrian's focus is the correct one, I want to talk not about politics but about the economics of a social contract. I take the issue to be the choice of strategy for economic development. The issue is not how to deal with inflation, but how to develop our economy in the face of international competition. For corporate managers the appropriate strategy entails not just restraint on workers' wages but, more important, an expansion of management rights—over work rules on the shop floor and over investment in the board room. It is a dangerous illusion for us to think that, via some process of consensus with management, workers can trade off a little in wages and get a share of management rights.

Leo Panitch made an important point that I want to repeat. Let us question the appeal, among many on the left in Canada, of the social contract in western European countries. Allan Blakeney referred to the allegedly superior unemployment-inflation performance of certain European countries with social democratic governments relative to that in North America. But during the last two decades average inflation has been higher in Europe than in North America for probably all but three or four years. People throw around the idea that codetermination brings with it higher productivity growth, but Japan has had rapid productivity growth without codetermination. People sometimes refer favourably to Yugoslavia as a country where workers formally control their firms, but the last time I looked at the figures Yugoslavia's inflation rate stood at 35%, its unemployment at 15%. Admittedly European unemployment has been lower than in Canada. The explanation does not lie with different industrial relations systems, but with two other reasons: the relative loss of dominance of the American economy and the technological catch-up of Europe; and the political power of workers in Europe. European workers don't have the collective bargaining strength we do, but they have more political power, and they have used that power to realize lower unemployment.

The world has changed in disturbing ways. John started off discussing some of these changes, but then he proposed solutions from the 1960s. In the 1960s, at a time of rapid economic growth, all political parties gravitated towards the centre. Everywhere, including in Canada, conservative governments were introducing social democratic demands. Now in the 1980s we see social democratic governments introducing right wing policies. The reason for this anomaly is, as John laid out well, that we no longer are enjoying consistent productivity growth. The industrialized western economies are internationally engaged in intense competition. That has polarized policy alternatives, and created political crises.

To solve these crises you have two choices. Either you strengthen the power of corporations to control resources or—what is a fairly radical choice!—you find an alternative to the corporation. Anything between, risks giving the worst of both: corporate shareholders will be angry, and the general public will not give wholehearted support. If there is to be a new social contract, you have to decide which of these two choices to pursue. If you opt for the first choice, to rely on private corporations and politically control labour, you cannot simultaneously promise social improvements. It's nice to talk about tax reform, for example, but if you increase taxes on profits—on the rich—then shareholders rebel; they go on strike. To undertake a regional policy that directs investments to the West or the Maritimes requires that you bribe companies to relocate. And where do you get the money to bribe them? From the rest of us. If you reject the first choice, you have to come down very strongly on the side of labour. That means restricting the power of capital and extending the rights of organized labour.

Many think of a new social contract as a cop-out from the tough choice between capital and labour. They think of it as something popular, that prevents polarization, and improves the business climate; something whereby labour are nice guys and business guarantee labour some rights. But you can't cop out; the choices are limited. If you don't want to accede to capital, you cannot avoid left wing policies: restricting capital flows, nationalizing the banks and other major corporations, planning foreign trade and the domestic economy.

Let me add another couple of points. Allan Blakeney wanted to look at the social contract as a process. Exactly! The first thing to ask about the process is, what is the effect of debating the social contract? It seems to me the effect is that people begin to say wages are the problem. Even if you try to dress it up, that's what it comes down to. You promise workers all kinds of things provided they agree to limit union powers to increase wages. You are asking workers to give up the most important organization they have for defending their day-to-day rights, not just their wages. If you are asking that, workers will want in exchange guarantees that limit the freedom of capital: guarantees about plant closures, guarantees to full employment, guarantees to social equity. If the NDP does not hammer away for these guarantees that take away capital's rights, the focus of the debate will be wage restraint.

Allan implied the two alternatives were Thatcherism as a conservative reaction to free collective bargaining, or a social contract entailing an incomes policy. If this is the choice, we might as well give up. That's equivalent to saying, well, the NDP's not going to get elected so my alternatives are the Tories and Liberals. To develop a serious alternative this group should get together to talk not about a social contract but about socialism.

Here's another part of the process. What happens to trade unions in our society when you restrain collective bargaining rights? Collective bargaining is basically what unions are all about. Progressive unions do many other things, but if you take away collective bargaining, they will wither and die. Let me give you an example from the North American auto industry. In the current crisis the American UAW accepted wage concessions because they believed themselves too weak to take on management, and because management offered other things in exchange. They offered job security, and they offered the union more input into management decisions, including board level representation—obviously much less than parity as John was proposing. In the long run these promises couldn't be fulfilled. Management had no intention of fulfilling them and, anyway, in a competitive market, there is a limit to what management can do. By contrast, in Canada we limited the concessions and got the best agreements ever at the local level. We got them through fighting, not through trying to make a consensus deal. You can't go to management and expect to get anything fundamental without having behind you the strength that comes from being prepared to fight.

One final point. For two reasons a consensus social contract entailing an incomes policy won't work as a development strategy. Because our economy is so unfair and the distribution of power so unequal, workers will in due course try to resist controls. Then, in order to put workers in their place, governments increase unemployment. That's why, at the time the Liberals introduced an incomes policy in 1975, they also increased unemployment by restrictive monetarist policies. The second reason is that wage restraint does not solve the structural problems that face Canada: trade dependence on the United States, foreign ownership, etc.

Elwood Cowley: I agreed with Peter Warrian for the first three quarters of what he had to say. Speaking from a Saskatchewan context, I am not so much worried by the relationship between the unions and a

NDP government—although there are obvious problems in the relationship—as by the relationship between the trade union movement at the federal level and the federal NDP. Many of us see the union movement restraining the party's ability to develop attractive policy. The major national unions have a central Canadian outlook— "save the auto industry and the textile industry" — while most of us in the West would rather buy Toyotas because they are cheaper and more reliable. (I'm not sure Toyotas really are better, but it's the popular conception.)

Whether we want it or not, there will be in the next several years a debate in Saskatchewan about the relationship between the union movement and the NDP. If the question is simply, shall we be aligned with labour? I fear the answer will be no. I obviously prefer to pose the question differently, how can we define the relationship between the NDP and unions more clearly? I'm not personally wedded to the social contract ideas of the *June 22nd Statement*, but we do need to have a debate about our respective goals. What do we want to accomplish? How are we going to do it? What precisely should be the relationship between the NDP and unions? What happens to that relationship when we form the government?

Forming the government is something the Saskatchewan NDP faces from time to time. That imposes a sense of accountability to the public that the federal party, never having been close to office, has never had to cope with. I view the trade union movement in a similar way to the federal NDP, as excessively conservative. Leaders of both can utter radical ideas, but neither have anything to do with changing the world by implementing them.

At this point I'm going to overstate my case because I want to get a response. I think the trade union leadership and staff basically like the present adversarial collective bargaining system—after all, that's what gives them their jobs—and don't want to consider other options. I mentioned in an earlier session the matter of union pension monies. While in Germany unions simultaneously engage in collective bargaining and own companies, the Canadian union leadership is terrified of ever owning 51% of a corporation. Why? Because then they would be responsible for making real decisions: whether to close a plant or open a new one, or whether to invest in new technology. Instead they avoid such decisions by letting Wood Gundy invest their pension funds at 5 1/2% guaranteeing lousy pensions for their members. Unions have no real power in our society because they don't want to assume any managerial responsibility in dealing with real problems.

There's a conservative tendency on the part of the union movement to stay with what it's got—to defend every last clause in collective bargaining legislation. Union leaders want to concentrate the debate on wages, and avoid difficult subjects like "quality of work life". When we as government in Saskatchewan cautiously introduced the idea of industrial democracy in the management of our crown corporations, union people were schizophrenic. The Saskatchewan Federation of Labour refused to say whether it was a good or a bad idea. Their spokesmen said, well, some of our unions like it and some don't but the Federation doesn't really have a position. Obviously, once you take part in a decision, you bear some responsiblity for it and, from my experience, the last thing union leaders want is responsibility for anything beyond wage settlements and grievances.

The union movement represents only a minority of the workers in Canada. Without question it tends to represent "middle class" workers. Unionized miners, public sector workers and even Safeway checkout clerks are probably all in the top half of the income distribution. The bottom half is largely non-union. There is a need for debate on how to help such people, but let's not cloak it in left rhetoric that pretends either the NDP or union movement effectively represents them now.

Here at this seminar we are not talking about the really poor; we are talking about the sharing of power among corporations, government and organized labour. To exercise power means taking responsibility. I think the union movement has a great deal to offer, as does the NDP. But we both are afraid. Let me give an example. Northern Telecom approached the Saskatchewan government on the location—either in Saskatoon or Edmonton—of a research facility. They didn't want skilled workers or ideas; they wanted money! We were afraid to commit ourselves financially. Ultimately, I'm just not sure whether we—as New Democrats or union members—really want to exercise power, and the responsibility that comes with it.

Don Aitken: I don't agree with you, Elwood. Some of us at this seminar have become victims of the "big lie" of the neoconservatives, according to which our major economic problems are inflation and union power. They don't have the evidence to justify their charges that workers are getting more of the GNP, or that unions are disrupting the economy. And the NDP, rather than defend labour, has fallen for the "big lie". If you tell a lie often enough, people will believe it. That's what has happened, and we in the NDP are compromising ourselves in order to remain credible with the people who believe the lie.

Those who want to be moderate liberals have a perfect opportunity at the moment. The Liberal Party is trying to reorganize itself now that Trudeau has gone, and anyone who wants to join should do so. On the other hand, those of us who want to form a social democratic government in this country should own up and say so. One of the things that means is to stop taking the blame for our society's problems. Damn it, they aren't our fault! In particular, unions have been the victims, not the villains of our economic drama.

Elwood, you complained that the unions impose a central Canadian outlook on the federal NDP. But you cannot deny the reality that the majority of the vote is in the major industrial centres of central Canada. Even were the NDP not formally aligned to the union movement, it would be suicide for the party to ignore the problems of blue collar workers in Windsor or Oshawa. Union participation in the NDP gives it a window into the industrial problems of the country. Without that participation the party simply would not be.

Leo Panitch: I want to take the discussion back to John Richards' paper. It was a considered contribution that goes well beyond a rationale for an incomes policy. Anyone who thinks John has moved to the right to come to his present position is absolutely wrong. John is doing more dreaming in technicolour than he ever did when he was in the Waffle! Do you think NDP leaders can call for worker parity on the boards of directors of major corporations of this country and get away with it? Some here have called the unions conservative because their leaders want adversarial collective bargaining, and do not want to get involved in management decision-making. Can you imagine just how adversarial industrial relations would become if a Canadian government attempted to institute such a policy?

No European social contract—not one—operates on the principle of parity on boards of directors between workers and owners. Indeed, a component of European social contracts has been that unions not step on managerial prerogatives. When, in the late 1940s, parity came to one industry in one country—the West German iron and steel industry—business successfully resisted its extension. When the Swedish Social Democrats tried to introduce the "wage earners fund", whereby unions would acquire equity in their firms over time, it created massive controversy both in the party and beyond. Were the NDP to pursue John's ideas it would create a great deal of adversarial conflict with business, and I think a large number of New Democrats would "flip". They don't want that level of conflict.

A little knowledge is dangerous. John, you know a little about Britain, but only a little. You refer to the Bullock *Report*. It almost split the Labour Party, but you are wrong to emphasize left-wing criticism of it on grounds of "class collaboration". The business representatives on the Bullock Inquiry objected to parity, and the right wing of the Labour Party baulked at the idea. Don't forget that it was the right wing "social democrats" who left the Labour Party to form the Social Democratic Party, and they did so largely because they felt the unions were too strong. They disagreed with the union demand, supported by Bullock, that the unions control the election process to determine the worker half of elected boards. There is substantial interview research to suggest that the reason the Confederation of British Industries decided to support the neoconservative Margaret Thatcher was that Bullock scared them.

When the CLC calls for nationalizing the banks, that is not nearly as revolutionary a demand, not nearly as adversarial, as parity codetermination. If, on the other hand, you are just saying, as Jim Laxer does, let's give labour a voice on some advisory councils, let's consult in quality circles, then you are advocating something not much different from the policy of the Ontario Conservative government.

Norman McLellan: I'm a vice-president of the Alberta Federation of Labour, and I don't remember anyone from the NDP coming to the labour movement and asking, what do you think of a social contract that includes an incomes policy? It didn't happen. This is an excellent debate, but the order of discussion is wrong. The first question should be, does the NDP want official support from labour? If it endorses an incomes policy, it will lose that support. I for one do not and will not support an incomes policy.

I attended the 1983 federal NDP convention in Regina. I got the impression this *June 22nd Statement* was made up by a few people in a back room without consultation with labour. You have to consult labour prior to implementing policies such as this, and that consultation just hasn't taken place.

I was in British Columbia in 1975 and was one of those striking forest workers legislated back to work by the NDP government. I dropped out of the NDP at the time and, quite frankly, I looked for something further left. I couldn't find anything else that suited me more. I forgave the NDP. The NDP makes mistakes; labour makes lots of mistakes too. But a lot of people will not forgive the mistake of supporting an incomes policy. How can you talk of controlling wages until you control the banks, the resource companies—all those with capital? How can you want to control workers' strikes without being able to control strikes by those with money?

Quite bluntly, I think this idea of a social contract is a policy to get elected. And if the NDP is going to move further to the right to get elected, then we might as well all join the Liberals.

Art Kube: Some say we shouldn't talk about an incomes policy. That's silly. We know that all incomes arise in a context of restraints and incentives. Of course we should talk about an incomes policy, but we should be careful not to equate incomes policy with wage controls. How in hell can you talk about equity in the system unless you address the question of an incomes policy?

We've talked about options for the NDP. I think it important for the NDP to understand what I see to be the three options facing the trade union movement. First, it can muddle along the way it is. Second, it can make a deal with capital and do relatively well—but for a shrinking number of members. We would not do anything for the hard core unemployed or low paid non-union workers. The third option is the tough one, to broaden out and make common cause with the disenfranchised.

To a certain extent both the NDP and union movement have adopted the proposition that we know what is good for everyone, and lost touch with our roots. We have both relied to a great extent on influencing the parliamentary system. When that system doesn't work, the NDP can't cope with extra-parliamentary politics. That's what happened to the NDP in British Columbia in the fall of 1983 when unions and other affected groups launched Operation Solidarity to fight the Social Credit restraint program.

I have a hard time talking about a social contract and codetermination on a macro level. Who will benefit by it? Will it be only a small group of workers in big companies? Maybe instead, the left must go back to its roots, back into communities.

John Richards: The term "social contract" is creating more trouble than it's worth. It's the content that matters; we can abandon the label if need be. I won't try to respond to every argument made in what has been a stimulating debate. Instead I want to emphasize the argument Elwood Cowley made: nothing fundamental will change in our economy unless and until workers and their organizations are prepared to play an entrepreneurial role in running their firms. Somebody has to be out there making management decisions. If the left ignores that obvious truth and spends all its intellectual energy trying to redistribute from the existing economy, it is implicitly admiting that private capitalists will continue to be responsible for getting new steel mills and pulp mills built. And let's not kid ourselves. So long as they do all the investing, the majority of people will agree—maybe not enthusiastically, but agree nonetheless—to private capitalists enjoying a large share of society's income and power.

To be frank I think most of the union spokesmen were guilty of ignoring that truth. Sam Gindin, I think you were most guilty of it, so I'll use you as my target. You assume the social contract discussion to be essentially about wage controls, and you oppose any change in the status quo until we have controlled the power of private capital. Admittedly you talked about nationalization, but for you it is just one more device to redistribute income from profits to wages. You said nothing about how the government should manage these nationalized assets. Somebody has to be out there making management decisions.

I completely agree with Peter Warrian that the industrial relations social contract as we have known it since the Second World War is coming unstuck. Organized labour cannot survive its present malaise, however, by a kind of "militant conservatism", defending every clause of existing collective bargaining legislation.

Leo, I think you are forcing events to fit Marxist ideology. You want to deny the potential of social democrats to realize significant change by evolutionary means. Social democratic parties often promise far more than they deliver, but they do occasionally come through. I may be "dreaming in technicolour" to talk about parity codetermination and I certainly did not say much about the practical implications, but I want to inspire people on the left—get them "dreaming"—about what is entailed in being entrepreneurs. We don't have time to debate European politics but let me throw out two facts. You claim categorically that no European social contract incorporates the principle of parity codetermination, that it exists in one industry in one country (iron and steel in Germany). You made no mention of 1976 legislation extending the principle to all large German firms, legislation introduced by a Social Democratic government with active union support. Second, I suspect both the right and left wings of the British Labour Party can share responsibility for not proceeding with Bullock's recommendations. An ironic footnote is that Bullock himself, despairing of the Labour Party, has supported the Social Democrats.

I share the fear expressed by several as to the potential of the NDP to really do something for the disenfranchised. Is it condemned to be a mouthpiece for essentially middle class interest groups—organized labour and farmers?

Finally, I invite people to ponder Peter Warrian's one liner from the first session. Labour and the NDP can't live without each other, but we haven't yet learned to live with each other.

Art Kube: I don't read too many economists, John, but I recall Kalecki saying the problem for labour is that workers don't save, and therefore to have jobs they depend on capitalists to save and invest their profits. It is obviously controversial when workers begin to accumulate capital. The Swedish Meidner Plan proposed to build up worker equity in private firms over time. The Social Democratic government supported the plan in principle, and that prompted public demonstrations, sponsored by the establishment, to oppose the idea.

There are some experiments in the direction Elwood wants. The building trades in British Columbia, for example, control their pension plan. If you want to get mortgage money from their funds, you must use a union builder. Let me tell you that, if a social democratic government were elected nationally tomorrow, the unions would be willing partners with it and we would agree to a social contract. I'm known in the trade union movement as someone who favours in principle the tripartite principle. I view it as an evolutionary stage. It's a way for working people to get information and learn the economic game. We would engage in the social contract however with the aim of fulfilling our responsibility to bring equity into society.

Peter Warrian: Elwood, you made four charges against unions. I'll reply to each briefly. One, unions are a conservative restraint on NDP policy. The fact is, the Canadian Labour Congress policy positions are to the left of those of the NDP. Two, unions are somehow not living in the real economy. I think we in the unions know more about the real economy—layoffs, conflict with employers, poor working conditions, lack of security and low wages—than NDP officials. Three, unions are schizophrenic about industrial democracy. I will concede a little to you on this charge. But compared to the schizophrenia of NDP cabinet ministers about practising democracy when in power, I think our union schizophrenia is much less developed. Four, unions don't talk for the majority of working people or fight the cause of the downtrodden. Well, compared to what, to the NDP? If you compare the historical record, or even if you examine polls on credibility about economic issues, we in the unions may show up poorly but we do better than the NDP.

Gerald Caplan: This debate has been as exciting—and as confusing—as any I've heard on the left. People have eloquently and passionately put forward a number of positions which obviously are in contradiction. What's happening, I take it, is that within the NDP, as in almost every social democratic party in the world, the consensus has broken down. The consensus on goals is still there; it's on tactics that we have a crisis. Sam Gindin talked about the irony of conservative governments of the 1960s introducing social democratic policies, and socialist governments of the 1980s introducing conservative policies. Ten days ago I attended as an NDP representative a meeting of the Socialist International. Leaders of the French Socialist Party sounded like De Gaulle. Leaders of socialist governments in countries from Spain and Portugal to the Dominican Republic find themselves undertaking policies of restraint. I don't think they are men and women possessed of less good will than we in the NDP. Events in their countries are forcing them to adopt such policies, and I'm not sure that, if in office, we would act differently.

This debate has been confusing because we started at the wrong place. We've made a useful start but I hope the NDP pursues a more consistent process from now on. Maybe we won't. I fear that Elwood's Saskatchewan NDP will look at a split with labour before all the logically prior questions have been worked out. We have to sit down and in an orderly manner figure out what our common bonds are again, and who our natural allies are. One of the problems here today is we're not sure whether we're all on the same side any more. I shouldn't exaggerate this anxiety. As far back as the founding of the CCF in 1932 and 1933 there were tensions between labour and farm groups.

As a party bureaucrat I would love the NDP to come out of the next federal election strong enough to have an orderly discussion on party strategy. But I must tell you that I fear, given political realities, that's not going to happen, that we will conduct our discussions in an unsystematic way and won't get the answers right.

Session Three: The Market Economy

Competitiveness, Productivity and Efficiency vs. Fairness, Equality and Democracy: a Discussion of Planning and Markets

Peter Warrian

Five Criteria to adopt

The criteria that should guide socialist economic policy are not difficult to outline. First is promotion of full employment—a job for everyone who wants one. This objective needs to be linked to a reduction in working hours because there has been a reduction in the socially necessary work time in our society. Second, we should seek the equitable distribution of work and income across regions, sexes, and age groups. Third, we must gain control of our resource industries, diversify our industrial base by processing resources further within Canada, and gain control of the Canadian manufacturing market. Fourth, we must insist on universal access—not access based on income or class—to shelter, nutrition, health, education, leisure and security.

Fifth and finally, we must determine, in ways that have yet to be adequately defined, the degree of openness of the Canadian economy to international trade. This is a far more profound issue than the simplistic "free trade vs. protectionism" debate. The debate at present is being (mis)led by those responsible for most of Canada's international movement of goods, namely the spokesmen for multinational corporations. We on the left must enter into the debate and determine the extent to which we want a closed economy or one engaged in planned trade. Either we speak out on this problem, or the managers of multinational corporations will speak for us.

Two Criteria to reject

It is more controversial to outline two criteria that should be rejected. First is international competitiveness. Here I agree with Art Kube. In debating a Canadian industrial strategy it is counterproductive to give priority to international competitiveness because it means regressive social and economic development. Why should we attempt to compete with third world countries where multinational corporations and local dictators impose starvation wages? Since the mid-1960s a process of "export substitution" has been occurring in a number of newly industrialized countries such as Korea, Taiwan, Mexico and Brazil. Their economic growth has been led by labour-intensive manufacturing industries exporting to established industrial countries. This process increases the share of exports and imports in the national product, making these countries highly dependent on foreign trade. I speak of "export substitution" to distinguish the process from the idea that economic development occurs via development of indigenous industries that substitute for imports. By installing massive industrial capacity in these countries, multinational firms have been engaged in a fundamental reorganization of the international division of labour. Given the scale of the new capacity, and the sometimes violent suppression of trade unions and other institutions whose purpose is to make income distribution more equitable, there is no way these societies can domestically digest the output of this capacity. The intended market is primarily North America and Western Europe. Inevitably workers and their leaders in these latter countries perceive the flood of cheap manufactured imports as a threat to their living standards and union rights. The main beneficiaries of this international reorganization—and major actors in the reorganization—are multinational corporations.

Let me express a word of caution on the fear of a rampant flight of capital from countries in OECD (Organization for Economic Co-operation and Development) to newly industrialized countries. There are limits to the cost savings from such a flight. In part from a reading of Japanese corporate strategists,[1] I think there will be a re-emphasis on investment within the OECD. But the firms doing so are only investing after achieving what approaches a concessionary social contract. They are obtaining from unions unprecedented commitments to industrial peace and co-operation, and from governments long run commitments on subsidies and tax levels.

The other criterion to reject is the preference for "high tech" over "smokestack" industries. There is considerable confusion about what constitutes a high tech industry. Classic smokestack industries—like steel, automobiles and mining—incorporate very sophisticated high technology. Further, there is relatively little net job potential in the high tech service industries, after you deduct the number of jobs destroyed.

Wage Bargaining in an Open Economy

We must of course plan our domestic economy and foreign trade in a context that respects union rights and collective bargaining. There is a widespread myth that high union wages are the cause of our trade problems.

Canadian unions have *not* priced themselves out of the market. Relative to our major OECD trading partners, Canadian wages have been falling during the last decade.[2] In certain heavily unionized industrial sectors Canadian labour productivity is excellent. Canada's steel industry, for instance, is the world's second most productive. The Japanese can produce a ton of raw steel in seven man-hours; Canadians produce a ton in eight man-hours. The Americans require thirteen man-hours, and virtually all other steel-producing nations require that amount of labour or more per ton. Nonetheless, the unemployment rate among Canadian steel workers has risen to 40% since the 1982 depression. The explanation lies in depressed world demand for steel, not in excessively high Canadian wages. Sudbury nickel producers are the lowest cost producers on the planet. Their costs are $1 per pound less than anywhere else. If international competitiveness prevailed, Sudbury workers should be enjoying full employment—not the 50% unemployment that has been their lot. The problem is not pricing ourselves out of world markets. The solution is not wage concessions.

Our wage bargaining practices do pose problems for trade and economic planning in this country. But the problems are not simply that wages are too high. The origin of our problems can be found in the economic strategy of Liberal politicians during the decade following World War II. Their strategy emphasized resource development and heavy reliance on foreign direct investment. One consequence has been the creation of circumstances conducive to "wage surges" led by contracts negotiated in the resource sector. Some people talk of public sector wages leading. That is nonsense. Public sector wages have never led, and probably never will. The direction is the other way. If economic conditions permit workers in the resource sector to obtain high wage settlements, unions in the manufacturing sector will attempt to use them as a precedent, and finally, public sector unions will follow. These linkages between sectors do indeed create economic problems in our open economy.

Having bargained on behalf of workers represented by the Steelworkers in the mining sector, I can describe how resource sector bargaining works. Frankly, you do not pay primary attention to wage patterns elsewhere in the Canadian economy, nor to the domestic inflation rate. What really counts are prices on the London Metal Exchange. If the price of iron ore, of lead, of nickel are high, you go for it. If the prices are low, it is a sober day from a union bargaining perspective. In other words, wage bargaining is tied to international commodity markets and has little to do with domestic economic conditions. Creation of a resource-dependent economy has created, among other problems, a potential for intermittent resource-led wage surges.

Consider Trail in 1981. Given high metal prices, we negotiated the largest wage increase in the history of Canadian industrial bargaining—an increase of $3.75 per hour over a two-year period. This increase exceeded the hourly wage level of many workers. But if we had backed off and settled for a $3.25 increase (as some suggested at the time), our system provides no way to transfer that 50¢ per hour to waitresses in Vancouver on minimum wages, to day care centres, or to retiring the national debt. To be blunt, either we got it or Ian Sinclair got it. Obviously workers elsewhere in British Columbia tried to use our contract as a precedent.

While our wage bargaining system demonstrates the inevitable deficiencies of being part of a resource-dependent economy, it is misleading to criticize it on the grounds that wages are too high.

What the other side is planning

While I have stated general criteria to guide economic planning, I do not want this discussion to be an abstract review of principles. We need to consider current policies of government and business leaders. After all, it is they who are actually planning our future. Here are examples of the major plans being considered or pursued by the other side, by business.

General Motors Corporation will seek to eliminate annual wage increases for its blue collar factory workers in favour of a profit-sharing plan. This is the reported GM strategy for 1984 bargaining. The company also hopes to reduce its unionized work force from the present 370,000 to 300,000 within three years. Further, GM would like to hire new workers at wage and benefit levels below the present union scale. Last year workers at the company's Packard Electric Division rejected a contract that would have afforded new employees wages and benefits of

$6 per hour, as against $20 per hour for employees on permanent payroll. GM management claimed it needed the lower paid workers to compete with wiring assemblies manufactured in East Asian low wage countries. Finally, GM is proposing to replace the three-year formal bargaining cycle with continuous "problem-solving" processes with individual union locals.[3]

What does all this mean? It means the largest manufacturing corporation in the world is seeking a counter-revolution against workers' rights and collective bargaining. In the controversy around high profile demands for wage concessions the media largely ignored other equally important management demands. Management has virtually destroyed national wage bargaining in the automobile, steel, trucking, food and retail industries, and has undermined long-established work rules, seniority and technological change provisions. These GM proposals would take the counter-revolution to its logical conclusion by virtually eliminating master contract bargaining and co-ordinated union wage demands. What would remain is the centralized power of corporate management to redistribute profits as they see fit.

The most pernicious consequence would be erection of a two-tier structure of wages and benefits in the workplace, a *dual labour market*. A privileged stratum of older, usually white and male, workers would be pitted against an underclass of younger workers, mostly women and members of minorities. Whatever the degree of segmentation in the capitalist economy at present, it could well be the death knell for unions if they become direct agents in further dividing the work force between the relatively well paid and the impoverished. Unfortunately some smaller unions, in rubber and machinery manufacturing, have already succumbed. Here is the dark side of labour's accepting a subordinate social partnership with management in the name of greater competitiveness, reindustrialization and "high tech".

An important aspect of the economic restructuring underway in North America is, to use Bob Kuttner's term, "the declining middle".[4] Taken together, demographic shifts, world trade changes, unemployment and—especially—technological change, have affected the job market. Middle level jobs have been disappearing. Production work is becoming heavily automated at a time when the most powerful agents of income redistribution, the trade union movement and public sector activism, are in retreat. It is worth noting, workers in the the fastest growing sectors,

services and "high tech", earn on average $5,000 less annually than
workers in industries with stable or declining employment.[5]

These trends make union commitment to social solidarity and full
employment crucially important. The most direct way to promote
equal pay scales is to promote unionization. When unions represent a
majority of workers, they improve the overall equality of wage distribution. When they represent a minority—currently less than one worker
in five in the United States is a union member—they reinforce the trend
towards a dual labour market stratified by sex, age and race. A minority
of workers, those unionized, enjoy a degree of market power that
generates rewards unavailable to other workers. It is precisely the
ability of industry-wide bargaining by a national union to equalize and
redistribute income for all its workers that GM, for example, is attempting to remove.

Paper Entrepreneurship

A persistent theme in the business press in recent years is the need
of North American corporations for a major influx of additional income
so they can regain international competitiveness and adapt to new
technologies. One flaw in this claim is that during the 1970s, the period
of our structural decline, North American corporations realized an
average return on shareholder equity of 17%, while the Japanese
earned only about 11%. For the four years preceding the latest depression, 1978 to 1981, the sum of corporate profits plus interest income
averaged 19% of GNP. For the four years a decade earlier, 1968 to 1971,
the comparable figure had been 14%. Admittedly much of this increase
could be considered compensation for the effect of inflation eroding the
real value of assets denominated in dollars. Nonetheless, if the business
apologists are right and investment comes out of property income
(profits and interest), there should have been a comparable increase in
investment as a share of GNP. There wasn't! The average investment
share stayed essentially static: 22% in 1968-71, 23% in 1978-81.
Furthermore, higher overall returns on capital are hardly justified to
increase Canadian savings which, if anything, have been too high.
Since 1980 personal savings as a percentage of disposable income has
ranged between 12% and 15%—double the U.S. rate.[6]

It is important to examine closely what corporations have been
doing with their funds. Prior to the 1982 depression they were engaged

in the biggest wave of corporate mergers in our history. Most public attention was on oil and gas, but the majority of corporate cannibalism took place in other sectors. And, given the stagnant share of investment to GNP ratios, those who were bought out obviously did not turn around and invest in new plant and equipment.

Corporate managers have been engaging in what Robert Reich has aptly called "paper entrepreneurship".[7] Through the 1970s corporate managers resorted to ploys to maintain or increase their firms' earnings without new productive investment. For particular firms this tactic proved highly successful. But since corporations were not investing much in new plant and equipment, average output per employee could not grow rapidly. The result was overall frustration. Buying and selling paper assets on the stock exchange became an ever more sophisticated form of gambling in which the real winner, as always, was the "house"—the brokers and dealers. Corporate accountants engaged in the socially wasteful but privately profitable activity of inventing ingenious manipulations of financial statements and a never-ending supply of tactics to minimize their clients' tax payments—thereby transferring the costs of government to the average wage earner. Ironically monetarist policies, by increasing the interest rate on paper assets relative to profits as a return to real entrepreneurship, contributed to the process. Investment in new plant and equipment was perceived by corporate managers as tying up finance for too long a period relative to the potentially quick returns from short term speculative transactions in paper assets.

Corporatism and the "Social Compact"

Robert Reich views "paper entrepreneurship" as both cause and consequence of America's economic decline. In his avant garde liberal view what is needed is an alliance of real entrepreneurs, labour and government against the lawyers and accountants. Reich, Lester Thurow and some other liberal economists are advocating a new form of corporatist social partnership, a "social compact" to finance industrial reconstruction that will restore American "competitiveness" and pre-eminence in "high tech". The now-familiar advertisements Gulf Oil has been running in major magazines and newspapers give the flavour of their position. The prospect is an explicit business-labour partnership to formulate an industrial strategy dominated by the private sector. This may indeed become the Tory's economic platform in a future government led by Brian Mulroney.

Currently the most important corporatist liberal in North America is probably Felix Rohatyn, Wall Street investment banker, friend of moderate union leaders, and head of the Municipal Assistance Corporation (MAC) that managed the financial bailout of New York City in the 1970s. He has been advocating a modern equivalent of Roosevelt's Reconstruction Finance Corporation as the basis for a new New Deal. In January 1984 Rohatyn, Lane Kirkland of the AFL-CIO, and Irving Shapiro, former chairman of DuPont, made a proposal on behalf of the Industry Policy Study Group, a body comprised of major corporate, labour and Democratic Party leaders.[8]

Their concern is to reindustrialize America in response to international economic changes which they view as permanent, regardless of the fate of the current economic recovery. They propose an Industrial Development Board to advise the President on industrial policy and assistance to industries in difficulty. The Board would be able to draw on an Industrial Finance Agency with $30 billion in assets drawn from the general public and union pension funds. The Board would make loans and guarantees, and provide other assistance to companies or whole industries chosen by the Board and approved by the President. As a model they refer to the Chrysler bailout plan in which the union made wage concessions, Chrysler's lenders forgave some of the company's debts and accepted easier repayment terms on the rest, and the federal government provided $1.2 billion in loan guarantees.

Interestingly the Group explicitly rejects "central planning" and the "picking of winners" by government:

> We have neither the capability nor the need for a single all-inclusive industrial policy.... The Board would serve as a mechanism for consultation with business and labour, and would help insure that government efforts do not work at cross-purposes with private efforts.[9]

The implication is that the only form of centralized economic planning will go on in corporate board rooms. Much of the costs of this reindustrialization are to be socialized, and corporate domination of government would be further legitimized.

This form of social partnership is even worse than the tripartism we debated in the Canadian labour movement in the 1970s. It identifies labour's interests directly with those of private capital. It also legitimizes the removal of government from the role of active agent and regulator in the economy, and threatens to undermine in the long run collective bargaining and social equity. It makes the public the hostage of private markets and corporate decisions. Tripartism was a European invention. This new "bipartism" is inspired by Japan.

Power and Participation

We have stated criteria for socialist planning and criticized corporate planning proposals. In my view, however, the key element in socialist planning is not the technical mechanics of capital allocation or of an incomes policy. The key is to express a social and political vision. This vision must include an image of the kind of economy and society we are seeking and the processes by which we propose to achieve it. If our ultimate assumptions are those of a centralized technocratic state, we shall never get far. We must opt for a participatory democracy as our form of politics, and the source of our social and economic policy. Starting from that principle, we can formulate some tentative conclusions:

* Planning must be decentralized.

* Collective bargaining, one of the only mechanisms of decentralized economic decision-making in the hands of working people, must be defended and expanded. No one has worked out a satisfactory view of the role of trade unions in a socialist economy. NDP governments in Canada have invariably come into conflict with the union movement, particularly in the public sector. Yet neither can succeed without the other.

* A social contract cannot be founded on an incomes policy. Control of wages has always and everywhere been the result whenever incomes policies have been proposed.

* Unions need more power over decisions to invest, introduce technological change, and train manpower.

* We should plan for more non-employment income for workers in the form of subsidies, post-retirement income, income entitlement for women and the handicapped. In Art Kube's phrase we need an integrative "social wage".

We also need a sense of what working people are experiencing. In the 1980s working people have experienced first a resource boom, then a depression, and finally a "jobless recovery". They feel fragmented and displaced. Virtually every working class family has experienced unemployment, has had a son or daughter go west or north to try to catch a small piece of some megaproject—pipeline, oil and gas exploration, coal mine or hydroelectric dam. Families have been split and stretched as people chased jobs from Labrador City to Faro in the Yukon to Fort McMurray in Alberta. They have experienced bust at the hands of Dome at the Cypress Anvil mine, at the hands of Inco in Sudbury, of the Iron Ore Company in Schefferville, of the federal government at heavy water plants in Glace Bay or Kincardine. They have experienced the crumbling of the resource-dependent foreign-controlled industrial Canada bequeathed to them by C.D. Howe and the other Liberals who governed in the decade following World War II.

Now workers live with a pervasive fear of industrial crisis. Canadians will be lucky to sustain the traditional level of industrial employment, about three million, through the coming decade. In the industrial sector workers face shutdowns and direct job loss. In the service sector part-time work and constant reorganization due to rapid technological change have become the norm. Telephone workers from Kelowna in British Columbia to Newcastle in New Brunswick are being displaced with new switching equipment that permits telephone companies to shut down smaller regional operations. The workers, if they are lucky, have a choice: transfer to a comparable job and leave their local community and families, or stick with their roots and suffer de-skilling and lower wages, or even unemployment. This scenario only applies to the privileged workers who have a job and a union contract.

Overall, people feel betrayed, dislocated and powerless, their expectations shattered. Politicans of the right are consciously manipulating their resentment. The NDP does not strike a responsive chord when its leaders argue their expectations can be fulfilled only by more government.

The crucial questions for the left are not ones of policy, but how to create a vision and then a political agency to fulfil it. How can the NDP become the acknowledged vehicle for political change for working people? The NDP is seen by many, including many trade union activists, as overly centralized and technocratic; or alternatively, as unable to deliver politically on its programme.

The question of political agency will not be solved unless leaders of the left deal with popular culture. As illustration of the problem, how many unemployed people did the NDP Members of Parliament, NDP officials, left-wing academics and union officials among us invite to supper in the last month? For most of us our cultural references are literate, high culture. We rely too much on the written word; we express ourselves in a manner most people cannot understand, and we do social analysis based on information sources that are invisible or inaccessible to most people. But there is as much, or more, knowledge about the economy in the bar at the Crown Point Hotel in Trail as in a university seminar room. There is more knowledge about occupational trends in the economy in a lunch room underground in Sudbury than in the expensive computer simulations of the federal government COPS programme.

Conclusion

A majority of working people believe that the world economy and, in particular, international trade and technology are changing. They believe that competitiveness and productivity are real issues, and this belief makes them vulnerable to management arguments—unless they hear strong arguments to the contrary. Thousands of young workers, women and immigrants know the segmented dual market as a lived reality, not as a construct of academic economists. Their frustrations at being barred from the benefits enjoyed by privileged workers make them ideal targets for the propaganda of the political right, such as the Fraser Institute, whose leaders can direct these very real fears and frustrations into mass opposition to institutions of the left: unions and socialist political parties.

For the left to succeed, labour and the NDP must be seen by all to be fighting for social solidarity, for workers' rights and for an equal distribution of work, property and income. And leaders of the left must speak the socialist vision in a language common to working people. If we can achieve that, then economic planning will take care of itself!

---

[1]See, for example, K. Ohmae, *The Mind of the Strategist: the Art of Japanese Business* (New York: McGraw-Hill, 1982).

[2]*Monthly Labour Review*, December 1983.

³*New York Times*, 19 February 1984.

⁴R. Kuttner, "The Declining Middle," *The Atlantic Monthly*, July 1983.

⁵ U.S. Bureau of Labour Statistics.

⁶Source of these figures is *Economic Review*, annual (Ottawa: Department of Finance, 1984).

⁷See R.B. Reich, *The Next American Frontier* (New York: New York Times Book Co., 1983).

⁸*New York Times*, 17 January 1984.

⁹Ibid.

The Dual: the Market and Planning

Richard Schwindt

I think an introduction is in order since I am a representative of neither a union nor the NDP, and am probably unknown to most of you. I am an academic economist, specializing in the area of industrial organization and public policy towards business. Like Peter Warrian, I shall be speaking on planning and markets, and you will find us in agreement on a number of issues. However, while he emphasized arrangements to maximize workers' benefits, I shall approach the planning issue from a broader perspective. Tentatively, I too argue for implementation of an industrial policy.

Industrial policy has become a major political issue. As definition let me quote from a recent article on the subject:

> What people who talk about "industrial policy" mean, if they mean anything at all (and some don't) is a new level of intervention by the government in the economy—basically, attempts by government to guide the fate of particular industries.[1]

For those trained in market economics that leads immediately to a core question. If you believe, as I do, that Canada's economy will remain a market economy, what can government do better than the market itself?

Some people look at the Canadian economy and conclude the market has failed because, in a country of vast natural resources, many are unemployed and poor. Others pronounce "failure" because, relative to other industrial countries, our rate of productivity growth is low. The governments of certain other countries whose economies seem to perform better than ours have used industrial policies. It is, I think, this relative failure of North American market economies that has excited so much public debate about industrial policy.

I want to discuss three options. The first is to muddle through with the mixed economy we have. The second is to solve market problems by a strengthening of markets, which implies less reliance on political intervention. Tentatively I advocate a third option, one that entails political intervention and which I shall define in due course.

Can we remove politics from the marketplace?

Undeniably Canadians have experienced a high level of government intervention in their economy, both in the past and today. The Canadian economy has been subject to some kind of industrial policy at least since 1879 when Sir John A. Macdonald announced his government's intent to industrialize Canada by offering free land to western settlers, by granting massive subsidies to the shareholders of the Canadian Pacific Railway, and by providing tariff protection to Canadian manufacturing firms. Currently, government expenditures account for 45% of Canadian GNP; the public sector employs one out of four employed persons, and provincial or federal regulations influence prices, output or the condition of entry for industries which collectively account for 29% of Gross Domestic Product.[2] Unfortunately, as many critics have stated, a good deal of that intervention has been ineffective. This is particularly true when the state has attempted to guide the evolution of specific sectors, industries or enterprises. Altogether too often, ad hoc policies have been implemented to avoid the failure of inefficient firms, or to prop up sectors in which Canadians cannot reasonably expect to compete. In some cases the public rescue of private enterprises succeeds, as with Chrysler, and sometimes it fails, as with Maislin (a trucking company aided by the previous Liberal government). (Postscript, 1985: The Progressive Conservatives seem no more adept at this type of intervention than were their Liberal predecessors, as the recent failures, after considerable expenditure of public funds, of the Canadian Commercial Bank and the Northland Bank bear witness.) And sometimes the result appears to be perpetual protection, as in the case of textiles and footwear. We have evolved a patchwork of public subsidies, quotas, and tariffs, which do little to reallocate human and physical resources from lower to higher productivity activities. In short, current Canadian industrial policy is largely reactive rather than proactive; it is extensive; it is expensive in both direct and indirect terms to Canadians as taxpayers and as consumers, and it is not particularly effective. What then is to be done?

One alternative, publicly espoused by a broad segment of Canadian society, is a diminution of government economic intervention, and greater reliance on unfettered market allocation. Despite the problems posed by markets, I believe market forces can in many circumstances achieve positive results, and government attempts to mute those forces often create worse outcomes than if government had left matters alone. But as a pragmatist, I conclude that Canadians will never politically opt for an economy based upon competitive market allocation. In the first place we have never had a free enterprise economy, and therefore have no tradition to fall back on. Second, we are so far away from a free market economy that the changes required would be drastic. Third, the most basic public policies which could move us in that direction—international trade poicy, regulation policy, and competition policy—show little sign of change.

The first argument is well captured by Rea and McLeod:

> Unlike Britain and the United States, we have no background or tradition of unadulterated liberal capitalism. Instead, our earliest experience with economic development was characterized by the relative absence of competition and the important presence of the state, whether in the creation of the monopolistic fur trade or in the heavy public expenditures on canals and the early railroads. Never having known laisez-faire, Canadians are simply not accustomed to the classical model of free markets.[3]

Second, despite the self-image of businessmen, Canada is far from being a free-market economy. A superficial review of the facts emphatically and indisputably denies what economic textbooks consider to be the most fundamental precondition for competitive markets, namely a large number of independent sellers transacting with a large number of buyers. More than 40% of Canadian manufacturing and mining is characterized by concentrated oligopoly wherein the four leading enterprises account for more than 50% of the industry's output. Less than one fifth of Canadian industry is characterized by a structure that approximates the competitive ideal. (See Table 1.)

These bare bone statistics understate the degree of constraint on market forces. The economy is riddled with mechanisms to shield private interest groups from the gale of competition. Manufacturing industries are protected by a plethora of tariff and non-tariff barriers to intra- and international trade. Resource industries have their exclusive rights to dig, cut, pump, or net their resources. Farmers have their marketing boards. Organized workers have their union tickets. Professionals have their licences to practise. Transportation firms have their exclusive routes. By whatever name they go—union tickets, import quotas, timber harvesting rights, taxi medallions, professional licences, exclusive route allocations, academic tenure—these instruments confer upon the holder protection from the market. And this protection is valuable to its recipients. A move to extinguish these rights is guaranteed to meet significant resistance.

Table 1
Canadian Industry Concentration Ratios, 1980

Top Four Enterprises Concentration Quartiles	Industries		Value Added	
	Number	*Percent*	*$million*	*Percent*
75—100%	29	17%	11,411	17%
50—74%	48	29%	15,830	24%
25—49%	64	38%	24,867	38%
0—24%	26	16%	13,851	21%
Totals	167	100%	65,959	100%

Source: Industrial Organization and Concentration in the Manufacturing, Mining and Logging Industries, 31-401 (Ottawa: Statistics Canada, October 1983)

Note: This table is read in the following manner. In 29 of the 167 industries of the set, the top four enterprises accounted for between 75 and 100% of value added in the industry. These 29 industries represented 17% of the total number of industries considered, and coincidentally also 17% of the value added for all industries considered.

The natural resistance to any erosion of an interest group's protection from competition might be overcome if public policy took a strong, comprehensive, pro-competition direction. To my mind there are three major policy initiatives which could be pursued—international free trade, deregulation, and implementation of a strong domestic competition policy. However, and this is my third argument on why we shall not move to a competitive market, I see no overwhelming commitment to any of these initiatives.

Unquestionably, wide support for free trade exists among professional economists. Economic models and empirical research provide a cogent and compelling argument that Canadians would be better off if trade barriers were reduced. Canadians have talked about free trade ever since achieving responsible government in the 1840s. In fact, for one brief period in the 1850s and 1860s, Canada did have a limited free trade agreement with the United States. Ever since, Canadians have discussed the pros and cons of free trade, and from time to time political parties have even advocated it, but the basic commitment of most of us has been to preserve our job, our province, our industry, from the ravages of "unfair competition". Whether they be academic economists in universities, government economists at the Economic Council, or conservative economists writing for the Fraser Institute, they nearly all agree that Canadian per capita incomes would on average be higher under free trade. Why do we not then have free trade? The reason is that the move to freer trade would, in the short run, create adjustment losses to those who have invested labour and capital in sectors that would experience falling demand. A combination of labour and business lobbies in such sectors has, for over a century, vetoed significant moves towards free trade. And it is my prediction that this combination will continue to exercise a veto for the next century.

(Postscript 1985: The free trade issue has once again come to centre stage. In late 1985 the Macdonald Commission[4] reported, strongly favouring free international trade. At the outset the Conservative federal government appeared to embrace the policy. Pressures have mounted, however, and from support of "free trade" the government has backtracked to "freer trade", and now "enhanced trade". The following quotation suggests the nature of interest group lobbying:

> In a development that may hold serious implications for the Mulroney administration's trade initiative with the U.S., Canadian industrialists are insisting on major safeguards, and in some cases massively higher government subsidies, before they endorse free trade.[5]

A second policy initiative is deregulation of industries currently subject to government-enforced constraints on prices, output, and entry. Airlines and broadcasting are prime objects for deregulation. The United States has experienced a measure of deregulation in the last decade, under both Democratic and Republican administrations, and there was hope in some circles that Canada, albeit cautiously, would follow suit. Certainly there was support, again from academic economists, and from potential beneficiaries. However, deregulation has moved at a snail's pace. Why? Stanbury and Thompson offer the following explanation:

> "Who can be against regulatory reform?" asked the Economic Council of Canada in its 1979 report, *Responsible Regulation*. It continued by saying "the evocative characteristics of the word 'reform' alone should be enough to indicate the side on which the angels stand."

> The problem, of course, is that all men (and women) are not angels. Some very influential people stand on the side of the regulatory status quo. For example, the presidents of Canada's two largest airlines, the president of the Ontario Trucking Association, numerous heads of agricultural marketing boards and the ministers of Transport and Agriculture have rejected proposals that would greatly liberalize or remove direct regulation of airlines, trucking and marketing boards. For them, dismantling direct regulation is an anathema .... direct regulation is now being used largely to redistribute income. Both the direct beneficiaries and their political "godfathers" do not face the potential loss of their benefits in the name of efficiency with equanimity.[6]

These types of regulations serve producer interests and not society at large. Producer groups are well organized, influential and clearly recognize their own interests. Consumer interests, on the other hand, are poorly organized, politically ineffectual, and fragmented by multiple issues. Unsurprisingly, the balance of influence rests with those who profit from the regulations. (Postscript 1985: The recent decision of the CRTC in favour of Bell Canada and against the interests of interconnect companies reflects the continuing slow pace of deregulation.)

Competition policy is a third area where reform might herald a commitment to competitive market allocation. Frankly, Canadian anti-combines policy is weak. It can deal with blatant forms of anti-competitive behaviour such as bid-rigging or outright cartelization, but it is impotent in dealing with structural problems such as monopoly, oligopoly and merger. This too is a policy area where academic economists have long argued for reform. In fact the revision process began nearly two decades ago, with an Economic Council study[7] calling for a strengthening of jurisprudence bearing upon both anti-competitive conduct (e.g. price fixing) and structure (e.g. monopoly). A decade after publication of that report the Stage I reforms, which dealt mainly with conduct issues, were enacted into law. This was to be followed by the Stage II reforms concerned with monopoly, joint monopoly and merger. Those reforms remain in limbo. In early 1984 Judy Erola, then Minister of Consumer and Corporate Affairs, tabled the most recent set of proposals. The draft legislation, introduced only after prolonged consultation with provincial governments and business, consumer, and legal groups, was a much weaker set of proposals than anticipated. In essence, the government was opting for the European pattern of allowing firms to grow very large and curbing their activity if, and only if, they blatantly abused their market power. This is a far cry from U.S. jurisprudence which can deal with market power, and not just its blatant abuse.

As it now stands, Canada has no control over monopoly, joint monopoly, or merger. None. Nor is there any strong interest group to champion this cause. (Postscript 1985: At the time of writing, October 1985, there has still been no action on the competition policy front. However the *Financial Post* has recently reported that "after months of haggling, the Mulroney administration and key business groups have come to terms over the final shape of a new competition law reform package."[8]

Industrial policy: a third option

If current ad hoc industrial policy does not work, and if there is little evidence that we are moving to a greater reliance on market allocation, what strategy remains? This brings me to the third option. If we are not going to dispense with government intervention, can we not at least make it more coherent? The point is not more or less intervention, but better intervention. The goal is to devise an industrial policy, in conjunction with the relevant interest groups, that pursues some consistent planning goals, and is not a series of expensive, ineffective, ad hoc responses to lobbying pressure.

The core element of an industrial policy is discretion over capital allocation. In a classical market economy it is the capitalist who makes this allocation, while under socialism the state does so. In our current "mixed" economy both allocate capital, with very "mixed" results. What is needed is a mechanism to harmonize public and private sector allocation—a mechanism which would, at best, lead to an effective, efficient, and coherent investment program and which would, at least, reduce outright incompatibility between public and private sector initiatives. Unfortunately, the mere mention of an "industrial policy" raises a red flag for some. No matter how packaged—industrial policy, indicative planning, concerted action, administrative guidance, promotion of national champions, or key sector stimulation—it raises the spectre of central planning and increased government intervention. But let me repeat, the issue is not more or less state intervention; it is the effectiveness of that intervention.

I believe that resistance to co-operative public-private strategic planning can, however, be muted through a careful selection of target industries. For several reasons the resource industries provide a natural focus for a first attempt at a coherent industrial policy. First, and most important, the state has a direct interest in these industries, both as resource owner and industry participant. Federal and provincial governments, particularly the latter, hold extensive property rights to both renewable and non-renewable resources in this country. Indeed the state has not just the interest but the duty to insure that these resources are exploited in a manner which maximizes the public's return. Obviously that return will directly depend upon investment decisions in the relevant industries. Also, the state frequently plays a direct role in these industries through crown corporations engaged in resource processing. Finally, the state plays an important auxiliary role through provision of infrastructure (e.g. hydroelectric power), manpower training, and in some instances resource management. In short, state intervention in these industries is extensive, traditional, and justifiable from the perspective of landlord, participant, and input supplier.

Second, resource industries are important to the functioning of the Canadian economy. Mining, metals, processing, petroleum refining, logging and wood processing accounted for $57 billion worth of value of shipments. (See Table 2.) Success in these industries would obviously have far-reaching effects.

Third, these industries are the nation's principal exporters. Shipments of metals, minerals, petroleum, and forest products accounted for over two fifths of total Canadian exports over the 1977-81 period. (See Table 3.) Fourth and finally, the structure of these industries is conducive to strategic planning. Co-ordinated investment policy is more easily achieved the fewer the participants, and in most of these industries the numbers involved are few indeed. Table 2 demonstrates that the major mining and producers accounting for a minimum of 90% of the value of shipments in each industry. Petroleum refining is also concentrated, as is pulp and paper making; logging and sawmilling are relatively fragmented.

Table 2
Canadian Mining and Resource Processing, 1980

Industry	Number of enterprises	Concentration Ratio*	Value of Shipments (x $100,000)
Gold quartz mines	16	94%	697
Uranium mines	6	100%	723
Iron mines	9	98%	1,873
Nickel-copper-gold-silver mines	18	91%	4,572
Silver-lead-zinc mines	17	94%	1,008
Coal mines	17	97%	913
Asbestos mines	6	100%	656
Potash mines	6	100%	1,046
Iron and steel mills	39	90%	6,432
Smelting and refining	17	93%	3,273
Aluminum rolling and casting	59	93%	1,049
Petroleum refining	16	85%	14,256
Logging	3,073	34%	4,559
Sawmill and planing mills	1,180	30%	5,278
Pulp and paper mills	60	49%	10,908
Total			57,242

* Percent of value of shipments accounted for by eight largest enterprises

Source: See Table 1

Given that the resource industries are important and therefore deserving of attention, that the state has a legitimate basis for intervention, and that the structure of these industries facilitates some type of investment planning, is it true that these industries would benefit from such planning? Richard Rumelt suggests that resource industries suffer endemic problems in matching demand with capacity:

> Requiring huge commitments of capital, the extractive industries can be among the most profitable in times of rapidly rising demand. However, products like sheet steel, paperboard, and petrochemical feed stocks are valued chiefly as raw materials in the manufacture of a vast variety of final products. Non-differentiated because it is their economic function to be standardized, the profitability of these products is largely contingent upon the balance between capacity and demand. In a mature slowly growing industry, the constant oligopolistic struggle to be a low-cost producer and provide flexible and geographically dispersed capacity almost ensures industry overcapacity (on the average) and poor profitability for all.[9]

Table 3
Canadian Metal, Mineral and Forest Products Exports, as Percent of Total Exports 1977-81

Total forest products	**16.9%**
Lumber	4.8%
Pulp	4.7%
Newsprint	5.1%
Total metals and minerals	**26.3%**
Iron ore	1.8%
Primary iron and steel	2.7%
Aluminum and products	1.9%
Copper, nickel and products	3.1%
Lead, zinc and products	1.2%
Uranium	0.3%
Petroleum and natural gas	8.2%

Source: Calculated from Bank of Canada *Review*, February 1983.

One reason for the relatively unsatisfactory productivity performance in many resource industries is the absence of investment co-ordination. Such industries tend to be capital-intensive, entailing large fixed investments (in pulp mills, mines, pipeline, railroads, etc.)

before exploitation can proceed. When many private investors and politicians form unco-ordinated expectations for these industries, they are subject to wild swings from unjustified optimism to unwarranted pessimism. The result is "boom and bust": an initial investment boom that generates too much capacity followed by a prolonged bust during which not enough investment occurs. That the British Columbia forest industry was subject to such investment cycles was one conclusion of the 1976 British Columbia Royal Commission (the Pearse Commission) investigation of the provincial forest industry. Far from generating excess profits, it was yielding subnormal returns to capital invested.[10] With variations, this critique is valid for many Canadian resource industries.

Compare forestry with petroleum refining. Petroleum refining has been a profitable activity over the last three decades. Until very recently it has not been subject to excess capacity. Admittedly during the 1980s the rapidity of change in Canadian and United States regulatory policy on oil and gas has combined with the worst depression since the 1930s to upset even the well planned strategy of oil refiners. How had the refiners avoided the inefficiency of excess capacity? To be blunt, they practised an "industrial policy", explicitly co-ordinating capacity expansion. They allocated shares in different markets and then supplied their respective distribution networks via a complex set of petroleum "swaps", thereby minimizing unit refining costs. Refining is an industry subject to important scale economies. Since World War II refiners have closed dozens of small refineries in favour of fewer larger refineries. The result has been less self-sufficiency for individual petroleum companies. If, in market A, Shell possessed a large efficient refinery, Imperial supplied its outlets with Shell-refined petroleum; it did not seek to duplicate refining facilities. In market B Shell purchased from an Imperial refinery. The purpose of this co-ordination was, of course, to maximize aggregate profits in the industry, not to lower retail petroleum prices. We may object to the distributional consequences, but this co-ordination has been undeniably efficient.[11]

With hopefully a different distribution of net benefits between corporate shareholders and the public, an industrial policy could accomplish a similar goal in enhancing the efficiency of an industry like pulp and paper. The claim of the state to intervene is highly legitimate. Provincial governments own the overwhelming majority of timber rights, and have an obligation on behalf of their citizens to maximize their return from this asset. Inefficient investment patterns in pulp and paper lower the feasible level of stumpage fees and other forms of public rent capture. Responsibility for past inefficiencies in this industry lies with all parties: with the managers of pulp companies overly anxious to invest during booms, with union leaders wanting maximum short run employment, and with provincial politicians prepared to award extensive cutting rights without thought to market conditions.

I am not suggesting that co-operative business-government strategic planning is a panacea for Canada's resource industries. Commodity markets will always be subject to demand fluctuations and no matter how great the consensus between private and public sectors, there will always be periods of excess capacity and periods of short supply. But performance could be much better, and they provide a fertile testing ground for the type of planning suggested here. Further, they are, for the most part, subject to free trade and thus whatever productivity improvements are to be had from exposure to international competition have already been reaped. They tend not to be subject to rapid changes in technology, and thus the problems of picking "winners and losers" are mitigated. They are mature industries, suffering in a sense from that maturity.

What I am suggesting is greater co-operation between public and private sectors to cope with economic change. There can be little argument that the current public-private strategy mix for dealing with structural change is woefully inadequate. Institutions have failed to move resources in response to changed economic conditions. Ideally, public and private sector decision-makers would have, either jointly or individually, the prescience to plan for changing economic circumstances. At a minimum, they should have the capacity to acknowledge changed circumstances. Unfortunately, not even this minimum is achieved in Canada today.

Essentially we face two specific and interrelated problems. One is to speed the movement of resources out of "sunset" industries; the other is to facilitate the commitment of resources to "sunrise" industries. Of the two, the first represents the most fertile area for collective action. This is simply because those who have resources committed to declining industries can be counted upon to petition government for help. Policy can either speed the exit, or impede it. The obvious choice is to hasten exit, and this should be done by providing generous aid to redundant capital and labour, particularly the latter. This aid should be tied directly and unequivocally to permanent exit. Adjustment aid should be decided upon as early as possible; eligible recipients should be informed, and a definite, irrevocable termination date should be set. Otherwise, "temporary" relief—such as tariffs, quotas, or subsidies—will become permanent. Some will baulk at the idea of directly funding market exit. But without aid, those who are hurt by structural change will do all within their power to delay or deter it. And given the political structure of this country, they will be successful. In the end, failure to pay off the losers immediately and definitively will end up costing society much more—either through market distortion or through social assistance. And, once a credible record of the availability and adequacy of adjustment aid has been built up, resistance to change will erode.

A strategy for "sunrise" industries is more difficult to define. There are two points here. First, government has not shown any special acumen in identifying winners, as the experience with Canadair, De Havilland and Bricklin indicates. Second, government must be very cautious when responding to interest group pressures to support particular sectors or industries. The current vogue for support of "high tech" industries is a case in point. A leading player here is the Science Council of Canada. In a multitude of documents (for example *The Weakest Link*[12] it has bemoaned Canada's negative trade balance in manufactured goods, and called for extensive subsidies of high technology manufacturing. The Science Council has gained some support, but has also engendered much cynicism among observers who see it as a lobby pleading for public subsidies on behalf of its constituents—engineers, scientists, and other science-based professionals. The Science Council has greatly exaggerated the Canadian employment potential in high technology industries, and the government has been wise in largely ignoring advice from this quarter. Probably the best policy would be for government to subsidize the availability of capital, particuarly risk capital, and to let the market sort out the winners and losers in the high technology game.

But this is not the place to set out a detailed industrial strategy for Canada. Let me end by simply setting out some general principles. For sunset industries government should strive to create an effective safety net. It must be generous enough to encourage capital and labour, particularly labour, to support and not veto economic change. It must not be so generous as to create a permanent hammock for low productivity industries. For sunrise industries government should strive to create a fertile investment climate, and then let the market do its work. And for those industries upon which the sun is neither rising nor setting, which includes the resource industries, public and private sectors should work towards a more rational allocation of capital. The choice is not between dirigisme and laissez-faire capitalism. It is between success and failure of the Canadian economy to reach its potential.

---

[1]R.M. Kaus, "Can Creeping Socialism Cure Creaking Capitalism?" *Harpers*, February 1984, p. 17.

[2]J.L. Howard & W.T. Stanbury, "Measuring Leviathan: The Size, Scope and Growth of Governments in Canada," in G. Lermer, ed. *Probing Leviathan, An Investigation of Government in the Economy* (Vancouver: The Fraser Institute, 1984), pp. 91-92.

[3]K.J. Rea & J.T. McLeod, *Business and Government in Canada* (Toronto: Methuen, second edition 1976), p. 335.

[4]*Report of the Royal Commission on the Economic Union and Development Prospects for Canada*, chaired by D.S. Macdonald (Ottawa: Minister of Supply and Services, 1985).

[5]G. Gherson, "Industrialists Favour Free Trade—On Their own Terms," *Financial Post*, 12 October 1985, p.10.

[6]W.T. Stanbury & F. Thompson, "Hurdles to Dismantling Direct Regulation," *The Canadian Business Review*, 1981, pp. 25-27.

[7]*Interim Report on Competition Policy*, Economic Council of Canada (Ottawa: Information Canada, 1969).

[8]G. Gherson, "Tories, Business Strike Deal on Competition Law Reforms," *Financial Post*, 5 October 1985, p.13.

[9]R. Rumelt, *Strategy, Structure and Economic Performance* (Cambridge: Harvard University Press, 1974), pp. 130-31.

[10]*Timber Rights and Forest Policy in British Columbia*, report of Royal Commission chaired by P. Pearse (Victoria: Queen's Printer, 1976), I, p. 50.

[11]See the Director of Investigation and Research, Combines Investigation Act, "The Refining Sector," Volume 5 of *The State of Competition in the Canadian Petroleum Industry* (Ottawa: Bureau of Competition Policy, 1978).

[12]J.N.H. Britton & J.M. Gilmour, *The Weakest Link: A Technological Perspective on Canadian Industrial Underdevelopment*, Background Study 43 (Ottawa: Science Council of Canada, 1978).

Discussion

Session Three

Sam Gindin: Richard, you raised the question of retraining people to move them out of certain sectors. But the obvious question any worker will ask is, where and what are the alternative jobs? Do you have faith that the market will take care of providing new jobs?

Richard Schwindt: The cruel answer is that, if government macroeconomic policy is such that the economy simply will not absorb all those wanting to work at present wage levels, then you've got a serious conundrum. But there are other aspects to the problem. When permanent tariff barriers artificially raise the domestic demand for certain domestically produced goods, shoes for example, we create jobs that have little genuine value to our society. I don't want to sound harsh, but retraining shoemakers to be hospital orderlies and importing more shoes might well bring more benefits to Canadian society—and to the country selling us shoes.

Peter Warrian: For the last fifteen years there have been approximately three million industrial jobs in Canada. We will be hard put, even with enlightened government policy, to retain that level. To create jobs for more people there must be a significant reduction in the length of the work week. Second, I don't see any net growth in "high tech" jobs. Where employment growth may take place is in the service area: health, information and education. A major debate will be whether that growth occurs under public or private aegis.

John Richards: Peter and Richard dramatized some of my own tensions on this subject. On the one hand, economists such as Lester

Thurow are too glib when they talk about closing down the "losers", because they do not address in any detail how the fired workers get other jobs in an economy where government is consciously maintaining high unemployment to fight inflation. In a high unemployment economy it is perfectly rational that unions representing workers in low productivity sectors, such as textiles, lobby to maintain permanent quotas against imports, and to maintain subsidies. On the other hand, you cannot have an economy with rising productivity and per capita incomes if, forever, you protect and subsidize "losers".

This brings us to the theme we debated in session two. If the "gains from trade" are large enough, somebody will ultimately realize them. Either some enterprising capitalist gets around the import barriers or, if we on the left dislike that prospect, we devise some alternative institutional arrangement whereby some group can assume the entrepreneurial responsibility for reallocating labour and capital out of low productivity sectors. An arrangement acceptable to the left may entail industrial democracy, or some form of government-labour-business planning. It is not an adequate position for the left simply to adopt the "conservative" stance of defending the status quo because of the risks in change.

Jim Russell: I agree with Richard in some respects, and differ in others. From my perspective in Alberta I don't see the evidence to support the existence of a free market with arms length transactions dear to the hearts of economists at the Fraser Institute. I see managed markets, cartelized markets, intracompany transfers. Given that, I see important areas—beyond the resource sector— for government involvement.

An area that strikes me is engineering. Major Alberta projects are designed and constructed by foreign firms. The concrete footings for the Syncrude plant, built in a region of discontinuous permafrost, were designed in Houston. The explanation is not that Texas engineers are better at dealing with permafrost than Alberta engineers, but that the construction firm had established links to Texas engineering firms. We will never break that sort of link unless the government makes capital allocation decisions, probably using its own finances. The irony is that the Alberta government possesses vast financial resources and doesn't use them entrepreneurially for reasons that are ideological, almost religious.

Peter Warrian: I think there is a great deal of mystification as to who they are, these economic "losers" receiving enormous public subsidies. They are not primarily shoemakers; they are Dome Petroleum and the Bank of Montreal. When the management of the Bank of Montreal makes bad debts to incompetent generals in Brazil, what happens? The government amends the Bank Act. The banks enjoy the best protection of any Canadian industry. And their spokesmen have the gall to make public noises about "irresponsible personal borrowing".

The economist Joseph Schumpeter talked of the "creative destructiveness" of capitalist economies as they incessantly invest in new technologies and discard the obsolete—obsolete capital and obsolete workers. In the eyes of conservatives, and liberals like Thurow, our economy is not destructive enough. Both share a cavalier assumption about labour mobility—that workers, their families and communities should be uprooted whenever technological change dictates. The only real difference is that Thurow adds a footnote that there should be some sort of compensation for the "losers" so they won't try to veto progress.

That displaced workers should receive compensation is I hope self-evident. The next question is, who gets to make decisions that displace workers? At present it is certainly not the workers in threatened communities. In a way I agree with Richard that capital allocation is the lynchpin. Who will allocate, and by what criteria? Will we develop new non-private institutions for allocation? I agree that unions should be involved in that process.

Richard Schwindt: Peter, in your address you gave an example of collective bargaining in the mining industry when corporate revenue was flush. You viewed the choice as straightforward—either your members got it via higher wages or Ian Sinclair got it. You couldn't do much to transfer that revenue to the guy making minimum wage. However, if the government pursued my idea and taxed away excess industry revenue during the boom, and reinvested it in some productive alternative, would the trade unions accept such a policy? In the British Columbia forestry industry three groups—the forest companies, the unions, and the provincial government—vie for the surplus revenue generated by the industry in normal years. I've never seen the unions moderate their demands and try to redirect forest revenues to government to relieve unemployment in other sectors. Maybe unions simply don't trust the present government. Maybe if we had a different government, they would.

Peter Warrian: On occasion unions have made such proposals. Fifteen years ago the Steelworkers, the dominant union in mining, proposed a mining fund, a levy on every ton of ore mined. The fund would have financed a variety of projects. Both government and the companies rejected the idea.

Tom Gunton: I guess any group must agree on some assumptions before a meaningful discussion can take place. But it is important to identify and evaluate those assumptions. Three of the assumptions underlying this discussion I don't think are correct: that something fundamental changed in western industrial economies, including Canada's, during the 1970s; that the left is in crisis because of its support for Keynesian economics which, under these new circumstances, is now endangering these economies; and that, in consequence, the NDP must develop some new agenda if it is to prosper.

Has there been a fundamental change in Canada's economy during the 1970s? One criterion is an acceleration of technical change. But John Richards' figures on productivity growth suggest just the opposite—stable productivity and a slowdown of technological change. Another criterion is major shifts in the relative importance of different industries. We might point to the problems of traditional secondary manufacturing industries, such as automobiles, but the relative employment shift out of agriculture in the 1950s and 1960s was larger.

Have Keynesian economics failed? Admittedly, in the early 1970s the conjunction of several problems caused inflation. Because of the Vietnam War's unpopularity the Americans financed it by deficits and not taxes. They created excess demand in the North American economy which induced inflation. Commodity price rises, particularly in cereals and oil, compounded the inflation problem. But what really changed in the 1970s was the advent of monetarism, a conservative doctrine that affirms governments can maintain price stability only if they maintain a low stable rate of growth of the money supply. Implementation of monetarist policies in major industrial economies in the 1970s created very high real interest rates, killed investment, slowed productivity growth and created unemployment. The problem is not with Keynesianism but with monetarism. Ironically Reagan has retained political popularity by repudiating monetarism and becoming the most aggressive Keynesian among American presidents. We may disapprove of his priorities for public spending, but massive government deficits because of military spending ended the American depression. In Britain Margaret Thatcher has also been forced to spend far more than her ideological colleagues would have preferred.

As for the third assumption, my argument is that if anybody faces crisis it is the political right, not the left. Monetarists must feel disillusioned; supply side economics has failed; Reagan and Thatcher have shifted policies. In fact, these two leaders would not have been elected without two random events: the Iranian hostage incident and the Falklands War.

Maybe the crisis we are addressing is simply, why has the NDP lost, between 1982 and 1984, half its support in the polls? The federal NDP is in crisis because in many ways it is an inferior version of the federal Liberal Party. I find it difficult to distinguish between a Liberal such as Lloyd Axworthy and Ed Broadbent. If New Democrats want access to power, they should have a social contract with the Liberal Party not with labour. The proposal of people such as John Richards for a new social contract would weaken NDP ties to labour and make it even less distinguishable from the Liberals.

Sam Gindin: Tom, you're wrong to minimize the changes of the 1970s. For the first two decades after the Second World War the United States was the dominant world economy. The European and Japanese economies had been devastated by war. The first change is that Europe and Japan recovered. Then in the 1970s some third world countries developed the infrastructure permitting industrialization. Technology has changed—particularly in transportation and electronic information processing. Financial institutions have become even more international. Profiting from all this have been multinational corporations which have established a level of international competition that is entirely new. The prospect of a multinational firm taking modern technology and combining it with the low wages of some third world country simply did not exist before.

You are right to talk of a crisis on the right; you are right to blame monetarist policies for some of the decline in productivity growth in western economies. But you must ask, why were these policies introduced? Not because businessmen appreciated Milton Friedman's theories of monetary economics. They were introduced because the world had changed, and many powerful forces on the right wanted a recession to speed up the ability of corporations to adapt and become more internationally competitive. They wanted to close down weak industrial sectors, and lessen the powers of organized labour. The contradiction in this strategy has been, what if all countries adopt similar policies simultaneously? We have an international recession.

We should admit that the right is being quite radical. The crisis for us on the left is to cope with these same problems and come up with an alternative.

John Richards: Reduced to its core, Tom, your argument is that nothing has fundamentally changed except for the aberration of monetarism; that people, including me, are exaggerating the crisis as justification for foisting unproved new agendas to replace the post-war Keynesian New Deal welfare state agenda; and that agenda worked fine in the past and would now if given a chance. Your argument is well made, but I think it too easy.

First, it is unfair to blame monetarism as the sole cause for the slowdown in productivity growth in western countries. In Canada the year 1974 marks a cutoff, the beginning of approximately zero productivity growth. That is two years prior to adoption of monetarism by the Bank of Canada. Second, something has gone wrong in our ability to maintain full employment and stable prices. It now requires unemployment rates in the order of 10% to achieve price stability, a level unthinkably high twenty years ago. I agree with Sam that we must ask, why was monetarism popular during much of the last decade among intellectuals, the business community and the public? For the general public, the answer is to be found in popular fear of inflation and partial acceptance of the neoconservative message on the need for more reliance on market discipline to increase productivity.

My third defence, Tom, is a cultural argument similar in ways to that of Leo Panitch in an earlier session. A generation ago we in the CCF—to put it in a Canadian context—comfortably described ourselves with the slogan "humanity first", secure that we defended the values of ordinary men and women. Now, the right comfortably assumes the mantle of defender of the ordinary family while the left champions abortion on demand. We on the left support a "big state", and champion "big labour" in its conflicts with "big business". Many of the voices for the little guy's struggle against bigness come now from the right. While some on the right are corporatist, others defend individual enterprise and eloquently attack depersonalized bureaucracy. Mostly they attack the evils of public bureaucracy, not those of private corporate bureaucracy. But, if you look at some contemporary right populist American literature, it attacks the Rockefellers and major banks in a style reminiscent of left populists in years gone by.

You are correct, Tom, to prevent us from glibly exaggerating short run changes as justification for charging off in untried new directions. But in my guts I think we on the left must respond to the problems raised by the right in the last decade. We cannot ignore their agenda, but we must define solutions different from and more humane than theirs.

Peter Warrian: Tom, it is tempting for the labour leadership to take the view that, but for wrongheaded monetarist policies and a few reactionary politicians, all could be well with the world. But the world has changed in ways that require new responses from the left. Let me cite one example. In the last two years the steel companies have dramatically increased productivity, reducing the level of capacity utilization at which they break even by 28%. That has resulted in layoffs, and weakened union bargaining power. Similar dramatic improvements in productivity have occurred in forestry and other industries.

My final point refers to Japan. Some have wrongly concluded that Japan's paternalistic management and lifetime job guarantee system has created an economy much more adaptable than ours. But lifetime jobs only apply to about one third the total work force. Even large firms rely on vast amounts of subcontracting to small employers whose employees enjoy no security. Don't forget also the extent of tariff and non-tariff barriers against imports into Japan. They want Canadian raw metal concentrates; they don't want the refined product. Japan is not economic utopia.

Allan Tupper: Richard, I'd like you to be more precise in explaining why you think resources the crucial sector for Canadian development. Your argument seems to be: this is the path of least resistance because of high concentration in the sector and a past history of government intervention. You ignore foreign ownership in the resource sector, surely a key problem in itself.

Richard Schwindt: I thought the name of the game at this seminar was to discuss policies for the NDP that are differentiated from those of the NDP's political competitors, and might just work. I see nothing wrong in proposing policy that follows the path of least resistance. And given the large relative importance of resources in Canada, I am proposing to grapple with the problems of a major chunk of the country's economy. Nobody can present you with a coherent all-encompassing industrial strategy. If I could, I wouldn't be here; I'd be in New York earning $500,000 annually.

I think you exaggerate the importance of multinational corporations in resource industries. In forestry, for example, the Canadian-owned MacMillan Bloedel has all the same faults as the foreign-owned Crown Zellerbach and Weyerhauser. The problems in oligopolistic markets—markets with a few producers each possessing some market power—are worldwide. Producers attempt to strengthen their market power by investing in new technology to lower unit costs. This produces overcapacity, low returns to capital and layoffs. Then, when some factor gives an upward jolt to demand, speculative processes lead to booms and above normal returns to capital and labour. These cycles disrupt people's lives and are an inefficient way to organize economic activity. The payoff from a more co-operative kind of planning by government, business and labour would be high. A related argument is that Canada is deficient in pursuing derivative research to increase domestic resource processing. It may not be glamourous like computers, but Canadians could significantly increase employment in resource processing. For example, relative to us, the Swedes generate many more jobs per unit of wood fibre cut because of specialty lumber, furniture, fine papermaking etc.

Finally, I warn you against demonology. There is a limit to how much economic events can be explained by the power of multinational corporations. Major corporations exercise power, but so do individuals cumulatively expressing their preferences through markets. For example, the ultimate reason that Maritime fishermen must leave the outports is not the power of the packing companies to depress landed fish prices, but the fact you and I eat less cod, and that the market demand for cod has decreased.

Allan Blakeney: A brief comment to conclude. No one should think it easy to regulate investment, in the resource sector or any other, or that the participants will welcome government attempts to do so. It can become acceptable to them if they have time to adapt and have some firm ground rules. The most uniform opposition to government regulation comes from general business lobbies, Chambers of Commerce or the Canadian Manufacturing Association. They represent businesses wanting the linked benefits of resource investment.

As a case study I give our own experience with potash. In the late 1970s we announced a ban on all new potash investments—by both private producers and our crown producer—until we in government were convinced markets existed for incremental production. Noranda in particular gave us a row, although with hindsight they are blessedly grateful not to have new capacity at this point when depressed agricultural markets have led to depressed fertilizer markets.

Session Four: Political Decentralization

A Critique of "Provincialization"

Garth Stevenson

While "decentralization" does have some favourable connotations—given my position some will be surprised to hear me say that—we are really talking here about "provincialization", something quite different.

I learned about politics the hard way. I spent my early years under Maurice Duplessis' regime in Quebec. I grew up in an environment where "provincial autonomy" and "protecting our unique way of life" were slogans to cover reactionary social and economic policies. While I concede that the content of Quebec nationalism has improved since the days of Union Nationale, "Duplessisme" is by no means dead. It thrives, for example, in Edmonton and Victoria where I hear these same provincial rights slogans. They sound no better in English than they did in French.

Let that be the prelude to my remarks. Four basic arguments can be made on behalf of decentralization:

1) By creating smaller decision-making units you can make government closer to the people, make government more manageable, and allow more popular participation.

2) The second argument, the "checks and balances" argument, is really an argument for federalism. In order to prevent abuse of power by some Jacobin-influenced group of politicians in control at the centre, it is better to create two or more levels and divide jurisdiction among them. Among political conservatives this is a very popular argument for federalism. The result has been, in all federal countries and not only Canada, that powerful business and other special interests have thwarted the public will by making the constitutional argument that some proposed public policy is in the jurisdiction of another level of government. For the left the checks and balances argument obviously has its downside!

3) The third argument derives from the idea of cultural diversity across geographic regions. If different regions are culturally unique, government functions should be decentralized to permit a diversity of policies to be adopted in the country, each policy corresponding to the majority wishes of the relevant region.

4) The last argument, similar to the third, is the public choice argument that the polity should be divided into many small units so that as few as possible are left in a minority position when a decision is made. The limit of this argument is anarchism. If every individual constituted his or her own government, no one need ever be in the minority on any decision. Some of the theories of public choice economists approach this absurd limit.

Of these four arguments only the first can in any way be termed left-wing. I have a certain respect for the first argument, but it is hardly applicable to the Canadian debate over provincial rights. Several provinces are larger than medium-sized countries of Western Europe. All of them, with one or two exceptions, have arbitrary geographical boundaries. In the case of the prairie provinces, surveyors drew straight lines on maps before the white settlers arrived. When I look at the performance of provincial governments—particularly for Alberta, my "home" province—I find it difficult to argue they are more responsive, more democratic, than the federal government. Were all provincial governments as small as Prince Edward Island, then the participation argument would have to be taken seriously. But then you would run into another problem: these units might well be too small to perform most administrative functions efficiently. A trade-off exists between participation and size of unit for many political tasks.

The checks and balances argument is so obviously a conservative argument against an activist state that, in addressing those on the left, little need be said about it. In every federal country the right has employed it to resist efforts by national majorities to realize social and economic reform.

The third argument, based on cultural diversity, deserves more attention because it is exceptionally popular in Canada—even, sad to say, on the contemporary left. The Canadian left used to view this argument with well-deserved scepticism. The left has always argued the essential political differences to be those of class, and that politics primarily involves attempts to reconcile class differences. The left has always been suspicious that cultural criteria—whether they be religious, linguistic, ethnic, or simply geographic—are devices exploited by the economically powerful to divide people, to prevent them from defining themselves in terms of common class experiences. Lougheed's Conservatives may argue, we're all Albertans struggling against Ontario; it seems very strange for those on the left to adopt such a stance.

A bizarre example of someone on the left using this third argument was Lorne Nystrom (NDP MP for Yorkton-Melville in Saskatchewan) opposing his leader, Ed Broadbent, on the subject of constitutional patriation. The NDP must distance itself, Nystrom argued, from Trudeau's Liberals; it must be a socialist party. Then he proceeded to argue that in Canada the real differences are differences of region, not of class. What incongruity from a socialist! Nystrom was adopting a classic conservative argument, the very argument currently being employed by Peter Lougheed, Joe Clark, Bill Bennett and Sterling Lyon. Empirically differences by class are more significant than differences by region. Apart from the special case of Quebec, which to some extent is a legitimate national community, the interprovincial diversities in Canada are not great. They are no greater than in the United States, and arguably are diminishing. Roger Gibbins[1] demonstrates that the differences in political behaviour between the West and the rest of the country are diminishing. The characteristics that traditionally distinguished the prairies—economic specialization in agriculture and multiculturalism—are ceasing to differentiate it. The prairie economy depends less on agriculture, and the rest of the country has become more multicultural.

Where do we find the most militant defenders of provincial rights? Not in Quebec or Nova Scotia which arguably have legitimate claims to cultural uniqueness, but in the governments of British Columbia and Alberta which have the poorest claims. Leaders such as Bill Bennett and Peter Lougheed realize, I suspect, that class differences are more important than any alleged cultural differences, and for that very reason are anxious to delay the evil day—from their perspective—when their citizens realize it as well. We on the left must avoid the trap of competing with the right by copying it. That can but deprive us of our raison d'etre. Thus, before we romanticize and adopt as ours the tradition of western populism, we should remember that Social Credit was integral to that tradition. Look what Social Credit has become in the province of British Columbia. If our party, the NDP, seeks to represent western regionalism and populism, it risks cutting itself off from the industrial heartland of the country where most of the working class live. It will become as sterile and reactionary as Social Credit became in Alberta after World War II. I hope the day never comes when we in the NDP think of ourselves primarily as the western party, or the eastern party—or the northern or southern party. We should be the party of the working class. Decentralization is like an overripe tomato. It looks beautiful at first sight, but turns to mush when you open it up.

There exists a fifth argument for decentralization, a pragmatic one sometimes used by supporters of the NDP. We cannot win at the federal level; let us abandon hope there, but by according more powers to the provinces, some of which we can govern some of the time, we shall increase the influence of our party. Supporters of this argument risk creating a self-fulfilling prophecy. If they transform federal elections, and campaigns in the heartland of Quebec and Ontario, into low priorities, then of course the NDP will never control the federal government. Ironically Pierre Trudeau, at the time he supported the NDP in the early 1960s, argued that socialists should view strong provincial governments as a blessing not a curse. (See his article on federalism in *Social Purpose for Canada*[2]. But the argument cuts two ways. On the one hand citizens of three of the four western provinces, Alberta notably absent, have shown themselves sometimes willing to elect the NDP. Conversely, the constitutional strength of provinces has been the basis for some of the most militantly reactionary politics this country has known.

In summary, let us be the party of the working class, and avoid the currently fashionable appeal of provincialism. First, because it is essentially "false consciousness", a deflection of popular attention from class identifications to spurious regional identifications. Second, because in a country whose economic development has been as geographically uneven as ours, it helps the rich to stay rich by adopting a "beggar-my-neighbour" stance on income redistribution.

I was interested to hear Richards argue not only for an incomes policy, but for provincial participation in the administration of such a policy. Admittedly he did not explain many details, but his scheme would, it seems to me, be an additional mechanism to perpetuate inequalities. In low income provinces workers' wages would be controlled at low levels on grounds of low productivity, while in high income provinces workers would maintain high wages.

Furthermore, provincialism shelters essentially backward elites who use provincialism to reinforce their own privilege. The protectionist policies pursued by provinces in recent years—preferential purchasing policies, regulations against interprovincial trade, etc.—are the result of lobbying by local businessmen anxious to avoid competition. As an aside, a trend that occasionally appears in the NDP—the pursuit of the mirage of electoral support of small businessmen—is one that I regard without enthusiasm. I note in the *June 22nd Statement of Principles* heart-warming references to small business, reminiscent of a Norman Rockwell cover on an old *Saturday Evening Post*. The fact remains that few, if any, small businessmen actually vote for the NDP. As the economy modernizes, small business becomes less and less significant, both politically and economically. Small businessmen are usually the most reactionary people you can find: opposed to unions, opposed to the welfare state and most of the 20th century. They make inappropriate allies for the NDP. It is not surprising that small businessmen cluster around provincial governments, indeed are often found in the cabinet chambers where they can adopt policy amenable to their class.

In Canada where much responsibility for economic development resides with the provinces, large multinational firms establish markets in which provincial governments bid for the favour of their investments. A perverse affinity exists between the multinationals and local businessmen who play a parasitic role, seeking to become suppliers of local goods and services to the multinationals. The local businessmen, in control of their respective provincial governments, offer concessions to attract corporate investment. How do the provinces compete against each other for the favour of footloose corporate investments? They do it by offering tax concessions, by enacting legislation against workers' rights to collective bargaining, by providing public services at prices below cost. One of the most blatant examples of this was the Nova Scotia government's amendment to its labour code drafted to meet the express request of Michelin Tire. The day after royal assent (to a bill that even the *Financial Post* described as the "Michelin Act") Michelin announced its intention to expand operations in the province.

I do not suggest that Canada ever will or should become a unitary state, nor that the NDP should abandon provincial politics. (I have even dabbled in provincial politics myself as a NDP candidate.) Obviously we in the NDP should use provincial institutions, like any other, if they can serve to make the lives of ordinary Canadians more humane and civilized. But if *real* change comes to this country, it must come to the entire country. We must address the issue of power at the centre, make of it a major priority. And when we are in a position to control the central government, we do not want it to be in the sickly status of the Holy Roman Empire when Napoleon put it out of its misery.

---

¹R. Gibbins, *Prairie Politics and Society: Regionalism in Decline* (Toronto: Butterworths, 1980).

²P.E. Trudeau, "The Practice and Theory of Federalism," in M. Oliver, ed., *Social Purpose for Canada* (Toronto: University of Toronto Press, 1961).

Decentralization: A Qualified Defence

Allan Blakeney

First I want to comment on the presentation of Garth Stevenson. His first argument was designed to discount the value of provincial governments being smaller and closer to the people because provincial governments are still large entities. I miss the logic of that. If you increase the number of decision-making centres from one to eleven, that is surely a significant change in the direction of creating governments closer to ordinary people. I just do not believe that the average citizen—in Red Deer, Chicoutimi, or Cornerbrook—feels as close to the government in Ottawa as to his respective provincial government—in Edmonton, Quebec City, or St. John's. And this is independent of whether he voted for the governing party in his capital. I suspect Stevenson's position arises because he has lived in provinces, such as Alberta, whose governments have consistently been to the right of the federal government. My position obviously owes something to the fact that I have had the good fortune to live much of my life in a province whose government has been to the left of the federal government.

(Garth Stevenson: More people have had my experience than yours.)

That may have been true in the past, but you are assuming it also true in the future. While a political meanness, in the tradition of Duplessis, may still be alive at the provincial level, be careful before you conclude that it is therefore wise to enfeeble provincial governments for the benefit of Ottawa. Political meanness can just as readily arise in Ottawa. A government of Brian Mulroney's Conservatives might revive the attitudes towards the unemployed displayed by R.B. Bennett's in the 1930s. The basis of your argument is that the NDP is, for some reason, less able to control or influence provincial governments than the federal government. I don't agree. I concede that the checks and balances inherent in a federal system of government can limit the ability of a radical government at the centre to introduce rapid wholesale change. Given divided jurisdiction in Canada, any wholesale change in effect requires double majorities—in Ottawa and the provincial capitals.

There is, however, an important countervailing point. How do we convince Canadians that the ideas of the left are valid? You say, until we can exercise power in Ottawa, we must content ourselves with talk, with political agitation; when we achieve power federally, then we can act. I commend to you the importance of example in political progress. Realization of many political reforms in Canada has come only after some provincial government showed the reform to be feasible. The list is long: Saskatchewan hospital insurance adopted by the Diefenbaker government, Saskatchewan medical care insurance adopted by the Pearson government, Saskatchewan no-fault universal automobile insurance adopted by NDP governments in Manitoba and British Columbia, and by the Parti Québécois government; British Columbia land use policy (Agricultural Land Reserve) copied to some extent by other provinces. Without a working example in Saskatchewan, Canadians to this day might well not have been convinced of the desirability of universal medical care insurance.

I want to contrast Canadian development with that in the United States. In my opinion there is no fundamental reason for Canadians to be further to the left politically than Americans, yet we Canadians have undeniably undertaken more significant political experiments than the Americans. Why? The key to an explanation is that Canadian federalism has preserved enough powers at the provincial level for provinces to serve as social laboratories, whereas American federalism has so reduced states' rights that significant political experiments can only emanate from Washington. (Admittedly some experiments, such as Bill Bennett's drastic reductions in social spending in British Columbia, may be of a conservative nature.) To launch a major experiment in social policy via the national government requires a majority of a parliament representing the whole country. That is far less likely to occur than that a majority of a state or provincial legislature opt for the experiment. When you talk to an American about medicare, he assumes it must be a federal program and then proceeds to talk about the problems: the inefficiencies of too large a bureaucracy in Washington, the resulting excessive costs, etc. Had a Farmer-Labor government in Minnesota had the power to introduce a statewide medical care insurance program, then, after a decade or so, I suspect citizens elsewhere in the U.S. would have insisted on a national equivalent.

Let me proceed to a second point. Stevenson believes that differences of class are, in some sense, more fundamental than those of region. I think he may be right. He went on to say the NDP is a class-based party. That is only very partially true. Again, I look at this issue from my own perspective, as a Saskatchewan New Democrat. In my province, if we had to seek election on the basis of being a "working class" party, we would have been long gone. In addition to blue and white collar workers the Saskatchewan NDP attracts farmers (who, in many matters, have the same interests as small business), teachers (who may or may not qualify as "workers") and a fair number of professionals. That description fits the NDP in most provinces where it is a party of consequence. Perhaps Stevenson's goal of a working class based party of the left is desirable. However that's not where the NDP is at!

From the beginning, at the time of the Regina Manifesto, we in the CCF and NDP have perceived ourselves, and been perceived by others, as centralists. Most of our rhetoric has embodied centralist assumptions. Slowly that is changing. It is changing because the courts have continued to interpret provincial powers, as listed in Section 92 and elsewhere, to be far more substantive than many in the federal NDP might like. But the courts do not operate in a political vacuum, particularly when dealing with constitutional matters. They reflect the undeniable dual loyalty among most Canadians to both their provincial and federal government. For example, whether right or wrong, most Newfoundlanders think their provincial government could manage the fishery or offshore oil as well as, if not better than, Ottawa.

Neither the "constitutional interpretation" nor "regional loyalty" argument is necessarily a left wing argument. Democratic socialists are beginning—I think correctly—to argue the decentralist case in terms of increasing the potential for popular participation in politics. Democratic socialists are lowering their faith in technical central planning. We are acknowledging the merits, not unqualified by any means, of decentralized decision-making. I am not a rabid "provincial rights" advocate, but I do think relatively strong provincial governments will abet decentralization in the most meaningful sense of decentralization to levels below the province.

Such decentralization is tricky; nobody knows really how to decentralize functions to municipal governments and quasi-governmental community organizations. Between 1971 and 1982 we in Saskatchewan made some progress. For example, our legal aid program was run by local community boards on which sat native people. Since natives are major consumers of the service, it was important that they perceive it as "friendly" to their interests. This aspect of local control has disappeared under the new Conservative government, and natives now perceive legal aid like any other bureaucracy run by the Attorney General's department. We made some progress in devolving administration of cultural policy. We achieved some innovations that increased the role of crown corporation employees in the running of their firms by, for example, appointing trade unionists to corporate boards of directors. Don Ching, as vice-president of the Potash Corporation of Saskatchewan, undertook some interesting experiments in non-adversarial grievance resolution and—with the ultimate goal of introducing elements of codetermination, of "workers' control", in crown corporations—he took a delegation of mine managers and union officials on a tour of Sweden, West Germany and Yugoslavia. By contrast we did not make nearly enough progress in making crown corporations responsive to the interests of provincial citizens, their ultimate owners. Simple devices, like development of consultative committees of residents of the communities in which the corporations operated or rotation of the site of the corporations' annual meetings, we did not use.

The bald truth is that many New Democrats are somewhat uncomfortable about serious decentralization for fear that local people will not make the appropriate left wing decision. We do not fancy the idea of a school board, after democratically consulting parents, deciding that the majority want no family life education in the schools. Nor do we fancy entrusting to locally elected hospital boards the right to set up or abolish therapeutic abortion committees. A publicly funded hospital should provide, most New Democrats would argue, all legal medical services, including abortions.

To what extent are we prepared to let go, to trust the electorate? This is not a simple question. I think, for example, of a battle royal with the Regina City Council. The Council majority favoured suburban shopping malls; we in the provincial government argued the need to protect the city centre. In that case we established an organization whereby the provincial government expropriated land for a downtown mall and, sure enough, Regina got a downtown mall. We acted, in effect, over the dead body of the City Council. Were we right or wrong? I am unsure, but clearly it is an example of a higher level of government unwilling to let go, unwilling to trust the City Councillors' judgment on appropriate city development. I conclude that many of us with confidence in our own judgment—and here I include myself—must accept that others have answers, and that the process whereby a decision is made is often as important as the decision itself. For many in the Saskatchewan NDP and, I suspect, other provincial sections of the party, "letting go" will be somewhat traumatic. But we must give it a try.

Let me change the subject somewhat to Richards' ideas on a new social contract. Can it work in a federal state? Certainly it is complicated, and there are few precedents. I am unsure whether Germany's federal structure helps or hinders realization of that country's less adversarial social contract. I am certainly watching intently the attempt by Bob Hawke's Labour government in Canberra to reorient labour relations in a federal country similar to Canada.

To the extent a new social contract involves an incomes policy, I do not think the problems insuperable. The policy would have to control only a few dozen key prices and approximately a dozen union contracts. In many industries key contracts set the precedent that applies across the entire industry. For example, negotiations at the lone pulp mill in Saskatchewan are a non-event. Both sides await the pattern set in British Columbia, and adopt it. For many years the IPSCO steel mill in Regina simply adopted the Steelworkers' Hamilton settlement.

If organized labour is to accept some limitations on its collective bargaining rights as implied by an incomes policy, there must be an important quid pro quo, such as public commitment to maintenance of a generous welfare state and to full employment. The federal government can use its spending powers to assure that provincial governments not curtail their social programs. Traditionally we hold the federal government solely responsible for maintaining a full employment level of aggregate demand. In our federal system, where the provinces and municipalities (which are under provincial jurisdiction) spend 60 cents of every $1 of public spending, I think we must insist on a measure of provincial responsiblity to maintain the appropriate level of public spending. In my judgment some additional public ownership is also necessary: probably nationalization of Canadian Pacific and its integration with Canadian National; probably nationalization of one or more chartered banks to obtain a public "window" on what has been a closed, cosseted industry protected from competition by federal banking legislation; probably nationalization—or provincialization—of a few more resource firms the better to plan long run investment and avoid typical "boom-bust" resource cycles.

In conclusion, I admit that implementing a new social contract in a federal state may be somewhat ragged, but why should social change be neat and tidy? Ragged or smooth, it can be done!

Discussion

Session Four

Pat Marchak: Garth, you refuted a straw man. I, for one, never thought decentralization equivalent to provincialism. I'm not interested in the fight between provincial and federal governments over their respective jurisdictions because I agree with you that this conflict amounts to a fight of the financial classes in central Canada allied with Ottawa against the regional bourgeoisies allied with the provinces. That conflict has been a feature of Canadian regionalism for many years. Duplessis didn't invent it and, in defending decentralization, I am not defending regional bourgeoisies—certainly not that of my province, British Columbia. I defend decentralization as an economic strategy; it is for economic reasons I am interested in it.

State ownership of major firms is a longstanding economic strategy argued by the left. As recently as last year the British Columbia NDP convention endorsed nationalizing the provincial forest industry. I suggest it wouldn't solve the problems of size: the oppressive, patriarchal and authoritarian nature of these firms. Bigness breeds insensitivity; it is the nature of the beast, whether privately or publicly owned. We must pay more attention to the fact that state ownership has never been accepted by a large proportion of workers. At a gut level they understand it would be to their detriment. State enterprises are run by bureaucrats—articulate professional people with experience at administration. And ultimately they run the enterprises in their interests; they can't do it any other way.

Garth, you say that small businessmen never vote for us and we should give up on such people. But what I hear from fishermen—and they are small businessmen—is not total antipathy to our aims but a fear of state ownership. I think that workers will mistrust all these new social contract proposals for similar reasons. They mistrust incomes policies, workers on boards of directors, etc. Such policies leave big capital intact, do nothing for the unorganized and, far from helping to decentralize, they further centralize power.

Rather than state ownership I propose what Bob Williams (Minister of Resources in the 1972-75 NDP government of British Columbia) has called a "devolutionary contract". It would be an explicit contract between the provincial government and those communities prepared to assume particular responsibilities in managing their local resource base. Management responsibility would be in the hands of locally elected representatives. The contract would specify conditions: they could not sell public resources to individuals; local labour must be employed; wage levels must be determined by the community as a whole; some portion of whatever surplus income is generated must be reinvested in industries appropriate to diversify the local economy. I admit there would be serious problems of co-ordination that have not yet been thought through. But so do serious problems exist in our present pattern of centralized resource management. For instance, the Department of Fisheries, planning the fishing industry on two oceans from Ottawa, is notorious for having permitted overcapitalization of the industry and depletion of fish stocks.

Grant Notley: I can talk with some experience on the subject of decentralization. My experience has been a harsh one as the sole "federalist" in the Alberta legislature until Ray Martin joined me in 1982. Garth, I think you risk posing the question as an impossible choice between Peter Lougheed or Bill Bennett, on the one hand, and an arid centralism such as we have too often displayed in the NDP. There is a third choice.

When I first entered the legislature, my attitude was similar to yours but I have discovered over the years that—whatever you or I may think of it—the majority of working people, as well as the majority of businessmen, identify with their provincial government. At times I didn't like it. Recall, during the crisis over the

National Energy Program in 1980-81, Lougheed vetoed any new contracts to sell oil and gas outside the province. Voting against that proposal was one of the harshest experiences of my political life. I became an instant hero within the NDP elsewhere in the country. But let me tell you, the comments I got from Alberta working people—from steel workers, from packing house workers, from provincial employees—they were negative comments. These people were not with us!

Why did we get such a reaction? Because—and here I agree with Pat Marchak—we in the NDP have ignored the lived experience of people. Perhaps the federal NDP's position on federalism— and I was one of those who initially supported Trudeau's position on unilateral patriation—ignored the lived experience of people in the West. As a party we cannot afford to dismiss the experience of western Canadians. The differences between Québécois and anglophone Canadians are recognized within our party, and rightly so. But we have forgotten that the experience of the West has been significantly different from that of eastern Canada. And because we have forgotten, we in the NDP have got into a lot of trouble.

Some of the western tradition is reactionary; some is positive. CCF and NDP governments in western provinces have been social laboratories that have altered Canada in significant progressive ways. An important part of the western experience comes from our populist traditions. Now, populism is not just a group of wild-eyed farmers in the UFA (United Farmers of Alberta); it is ordinary people insisting on having their say. I even see elements of populism among you university academics, Garth, when you get riled up! Peter Lougheed has succeeded for the last fifteen years in stealing the populist agenda in this province, but that does not mean populism is without relevance for us on the left. On this issue we must be careful not to simplify.

I want to agree with Pat that decentralization is much more than shifting powers from Ottawa to Edmonton, Regina or some other provincial capital. Although there are many difficulties in devolving power to local communities, there are good examples. My riding is adjacent to Fort St. John, Dawson Creek and other communities in the Peace River region of British Columbia. The community resource boards initiated by the NDP in that province between 1972 and 1975 increased local participation in the provision of social services, and increased the quality of service.

In conclusion, I insist that decentralization is not a stalking horse for right wingers. There are as many conservatives anxious to preserve central authority as there are socialists similarly inclined. When the federal Liberals toy with including the right to own private property in the constitution, that is in response to a conservative lobby. This lobby wants the federal government to prevent henceforth democratically elected legislatures—at any level of government—from interfering with the economy. They're not worried about the property of the average little guy; they're worried about the freedom to manoeuvre of corporate shareholders.

Don Kerr: When I hear talk of decentralization, I think of it quite differently from those who have spoken so far. I think of it in terms of people as individuals at the bottom looking up. Decentralization means the ability of people to form all kinds of little groups. Their happiness, and the sense of power they have over their lives, depend on these groups. Some of these groups are more or less political—a local constituency association of a political party, a union local, a neighbourhood protection committee, an ecology society. But many others are cultural, and organized primarily for the pleasure of their members. We in the NDP must take into account the extent to which people have already "decentralized" into their own groups. When the NDP loses office, as happened in Saskatchewan, it is clearly a setback from a certain perspective, but many people who operate at a humble level do not feel a loss provided the immediate groups in which they live are succeeding. I would conclude by emphasizing Allan Blakeney's point: it is important for the NDP to devolve more provincial power and, I would add, money to such small groups, and guarantee them as much independence as possible.

Art Kube: I passed my formative years in Austria, a unitary state, and always thought problems could be resolved from the centre. In the last ten years I've changed my mind. Many Canadians feel a sort of hopelessness, an inability to do anything against major corporations or big government. Even if you put aside the matter of Quebec, distances are just too large for it to be desirable to govern Canada as a unitary state. If a citizen in Terrace, in northern British Columbia, has a problem, it takes too long to get an answer from Ottawa, or even from Victoria, and when the answer comes, it quite often fails to take into account local peculiarities. The answer should come from a local government.

Naive as it sounds, people want some control over their lives. As the defenders of "big government", we're being outflanked by the right on this theme. Big government is inevitably an unresponsive institution. There can be compromise in which the federal government establishes national standards but leaves administration to local government. For example, the federal government legislates criminal law, while provincial governments run the court system. The provincial government need not always be involved. We need more direct links between the federal government and municipal governments on problems such as job search for the unemployed.

Pat, I want to comment briefly on your "small is beautiful" position. We in the union movement are not opposed to it, but be careful. People don't particularly like change so, when you talk about giving power to smaller units you better be sure that it will not mean massive upheaval to people and destruction of organizations, such as unions, that protect what they already have.

Davis Swan: I want to recognize the "good and the bad" of small and large scale business. Small businesses in general operate in more competitive markets than large. Small businessmen may be eking out a living, and this will cause them to underpay and overwork their employees. On the other hand, Pat is right to talk of size creating inertia regardless whether ownership is private or public. As an engineer who has done the same job for the federal government and a multinational oil company, I can testify to that.

I am sympathetic to Garth's frustrations with small businessmen, but I suggest two reasons why we should not abandon them. First is the matter of government's ability to exercise democratic control over the economy. If the president of Last Chance Oil and Gas says he wants lower royalties, we can as a government say, go to hell. If the president of Mammoth Oil (Canada) Incorporated says he wants lower royalties and will lay off 10,000 workers if he doesn't get his way, then we in government must accommodate him. Second is that, despite the self-delusion and unattractive greed of some small businessmen, small business does afford a measure of self-determination, independence and flexibility to those involved. One aspect of wanting control over your life is wanting to be your own boss. As socialists we should support that sentiment.

The major problem in our supporting small business is that thereby we are supporting the accumulation of private capital. Let's not try to deflect that problem. If these small businesses succeed, some will become big and then what? How do we redistribute income arising from private capital, and how do we make its owners socially accountable? That's where the profit-sharing and industrial democracy components of the new social contract are important.

Garth Stevenson: I would like to respond to some of the points raised, starting with Allan Blakeney's. I did not say that the NDP must wait until it controls the federal government before attempting to do anything. Where there have been provincial NDP governments, there have been significant social reforms. But nearly all NDP achievements have been in the areas of health, welfare and cultural matters, and not in the area of economic development. It is in the area of economic development that the limitations of a federal state with strong provincial governments become visible. We cannot ever equalize income or economic power in Canada by building economic barriers between provinces. Provincial protectionism will serve essentially to protect local economic elite ,. Those who pay will be working people across the country.

Nor did I say the NDP is a class party in terms of those who vote for it. I might wish it otherwise but the majority of Canadian workers don't support it, and many people vote for it who could not, by any reasonable definition, be included in the working class. Nonetheless the fundamental goal of a party of the left is a more egalitarian society, and we cannot achieve it by organizing people on the basis of some spurious identification as Albertans or Manitobans. Regional cleavages are not the really significant ones in society.

Grant Notley referred to the anti-centralist sentiments of Albertans, including working people. I congratulate Grant, as a one-man caucus, courageously defying some of the more antediluvian aspects of popular sentiment. The point is, there's a limit beyond which we in the NDP simply cannot support whatever happens to be the momentary majority sentiment. There are all sorts of majorities that we don't want to support: the majority in favour of capital punishment, the majority that is hostile to unions.

To digress briefly, I'll never forget one door-knocking experience I had, admittedly in Ontario not Alberta. I was canvassing for the NDP at a time when Stuart Smith, a Jew, was leader of the Ontario Liberal Party. I knocked at the door of a destitute house. A man, unshaved for four days, came to the door and invited me into the one room in which he lived. You've got my vote this time, he said. I always voted Liberal, but never again. You know, their leader is a Jew! I'm ashamed to admit it, but I didn't attack his anti-Semitism. Irrational public attitudes exist, and the powerful exploit them to create external scapegoats as the source of people's problems. It may be fair enough for us in Alberta to attack the federal government, but not to attack ordinary people who happen to live in other provinces.

Last, I want to elaborate on something Art Kube raised, direct links between the federal and municipal governments. I think we in the NDP have underestimated the potential importance of municipal government. In the United States, of course, the federal government has those links. They are an important reason in explaining a situation that Allan Blakeney deplores—the weakness of American states compared to Canadian provinces. In a way American federalism is more decentralized because it is more centralized! Because of its power Washington can create federal-municipal links, which weaken state power but strengthen the cities. Decentralization is a complex notion.

Fred Engelmann: I have been asked to close this seminar. It has been a stimulating intellectual exchange between labour and NDP leaders, between social democrats and socialists, between those of us in the hinterlands and those of you at the centre. Predictably we all opposed wage controls and to that extent the debate on a new social contract was not exactly a debate. But the idea of a new social contract, however incomplete our present definition, allowed us to explore many vital questions for Canadians. I think we brought our best to this meeting. Gatherings such as this are rare, too rare.

Postscripts

Attitudes Towards Unions and Worker Participation in Management

John Richards & Gary Mauser

What do people think of unions? Do they blame unions for unemployment? What do people think of present labour legislation, and of recent changes (by the provincial government in British Columbia) to limit union power? Do workers want more influence over decisions at work, or are they satisfied to let managers manage? Do Canadians want some form of codetermination (the right of workers to elect members to the boards of directors of large firms)? Or do they fear it will weaken workers' positions in collective bargaining? Do the attitudes of union members on these questions differ from those of non-union workers? Do attitudes differ among supporters of different parties, between men and women?

These are some of the obvious questions to pose before deciding what ought to be in any new social contract. The survey discussed here provides some answers. It was conducted by telephoning 335 randomly selected adults in the greater Vancouver region, during March and April of 1985. In order to assess attitudes by different groups, we asked respondents questions about their employment status, union membership, voting history in the last provincial and federal elections, age, education and sex.[1]

Some important caveats are in order. Survey respondents are all in one region of one province. British Columbia is probably the most polarized on these issues of any Canadian province, and results should not be extrapolated across the country. Other sources of potential bias should be noted. Sample numbers are small in some categories, implying large margins of error. The interviewers and the wording of questions can induce bias. Respondents were given hypothetical questions. Faced with an actual decision in the real world they may behave differently from their stated intentions. For these and other reasons one must be cautious in interpreting the validity of results.[2]

Before we proceed, let us address the instinctive mistrust of polling felt by many on the left. Results can be biased, and many complex issues simply cannot be formulated in polls. Exclusive access to survey results by political insiders admittedly increases the inequality of knowledge and power in politics. It is also true that surveys can at best only ascertain public responses at a particular time, that public attitudes change, and that we on the left have comprehensive programs we want to implement without constant reference to every fluctuation in attitude. At best, surveys can assess only imperfectly the degree of conviction by which people hold their positions. It is easy to say yes or no to questions about which you have little immediate concern. But any technique for assessing public opinion—from straw votes at public meetings, to back-bench politicians who glean the consensus along coffee row—displays biases. And these biases are usually worse than those from systematic polling. As democrats who believe in "government by the people", it is surely inconsistent for us to oppose polling in principle when the technique allows us to find out what people think more efficiently than before. With polling as with so much new technology, the appropriate response is not to dismiss it but to control it democratically, and distribute the benefits equitably.

The conclusions that emerge from this survey can be quickly summarized in four points. After stating the conclusions, we shall discuss each in turn. (Actual statistical results, and the questions posed, are available in an appendix to this article.)

1) *A majority of those sampled think unions a necessary counter to the power of employers.* The majority clearly prefer the present situation, whereby government regulates union powers to bargain collectively, to one in which individual workers and employers are free to "do what they want". On the controversial subject of the powers of public sector unions a majority are prepared to afford at least a limited right to strike.

2) *However people have only limited confidence in current union leaders and strategies.* Predictably, union members and NDP supporters give more pro-union responses than the average Canadian, but the level of anti-union responses is remarkably high among these groups as well.

3) *Workers want more influence over decisions of all kinds at work.* Being a union member, with access to collective bargaining, does not apparently lessen the degree of frustration over the extent of influence presently exercised.

4) *As a means to exercise more influence a large majority of people favour codetermination.* The majority is nearly as large among supporters of right wing parties (federal Conservatives and provincial Social Credit) as

among NDP supporters, nearly as large among non-unionized as un-ionized workers.

Unions as a countervailing power

Overall, seven out of ten agree that unions are necessary to counter the power of employers in determining wages and working conditions (question #6). Four of five union workers agree, as do two of three non-union workers. Two thirds of the sample also think unions necessary to prevent arbitrary favouritism by management (#10). Union members are a good deal more convinced of this argument than non-union members.

Some neoconservatives express a nostalgic desire for a return to the early 19th century, when the common law prohibition against restraint of trade made organization of a union a potentially illegal act, regardless of what the union did. A clear majority of our sample reject such ideas, and consider workers would be at a disadvantage without government legislation to define union powers in collective bargaining (#12).

The right of workers collectively to withdraw services from an employer, i.e. to strike, is absolutely central if unions are to be an effective countervailing power. The most contentious current application of this principle is to public sector workers. But even here a majority support the principle of at least a limited right to strike (#16, #17). A quarter of those sampled admittedly disagree strongly with granting public sector workers the right to strike. Another positive result for unions is the majority conviction that the growth of unions has contributed to Canadian democracy (#4). Again, nearly one in four strongly disagree with this conclusion.

Evidence of limited confidence in union leaders and strategies

We began the survey with three questions drawn directly from a major national polling firm, Decima Research,[3] bearing on confidence in leaders of major institutions (#1 – #3). Our results are similar to theirs. Four out of nine sampled express "hardly any confidence" in union leaders, as opposed to only one in ten expressing a "great deal of confidence". Among union members the results are only somewhat less dismal. One union member in three has "hardly any confidence" in his leaders; this compares with only one in six who expresses "a great deal of confidence". Among NDP supporters in the 1984 federal election a large majority, seven out of ten, express "only some confidence"; equal numbers, one in eight, express either a "great deal" or "hardly any confidence" in union leaders. By comparison, the leaders of multinational corporations and banks have generated a far more favourable image.

In order to compare our results with Decima we copied exactly the wording of their question. Unfortunately use of the word "confidence" creates an ambiguity. Respondents could reasonably interpret the word to mean either "approval" or "competence". Thus the results may indicate either that people disapprove what union leaders are doing or that they think them incompetent at the task of union leadership—regardless how they evaluate current union activities. The answers to another question, do union leaders represent the best interests of their members? (#7) provide additional evidence on the image of union leaders. By a small majority those sampled think they do not; by an equally small majority union members think their leaders do.

Question #5 illustrates a major difficulty faced by the left in pressing the problem of high unemployment. Two thirds of those sampled link union demands to the existence of unemployment. While the proportion of non-union workers making the link exceeds that for unionized workers, nonetheless a small majority of the latter also make the link. The troubling implication from this question is that people may interpret legislation to limit union power as at least a partial solution to unemployment. Those who supported the NDP, both in the 1983 provincial and 1984 federal elections, stand out as the only group in which a majority, albeit a slim majority, disagree that the link exists.

Elsewhere in this volume the argument has been made (see Chapter V) that many of the basic components of the present industrial relations social contract, as embodied in the Wagner Act and its Canadian counterparts, lack public support. This survey provides evidence to that effect. The fact that a substantial majority of both union and non-union workers want more direct government intervention to end strikes and lockouts suggests an obvious lack of commitment to the present institutions of collective bargaining (#18). Of course this is a hypothetical question. When on strike themselves union workers usually oppose such intervention. The public response to particular strikes changes, depending on the specific circumstances.

Other questions provide evidence on specific industrial relations practices. A sizeable majority of unionized workers, and a very large majority of non-unionized workers, apparently oppose the principle of the union shop. They want workers to be individually free to decide whether or not to join the union at their place of work (#8). Responses to this issue can vary considerably depending on wording of the statement; to that extent the result must be interpreted cautiously. A more pro-union response might have been elicited with the following wording: "Given that a majority of workers have democratically chosen to form a union, those workers who disagreed should be free to decide whether or not to join". A sizeable majority of both unionized and non-unionized workers say they want merit to supersede seniority in determining layoffs (#9). Again, interpretation of this result must be cautious; it is hard to disagree with keeping the "best person" on the job. For fear that employers abuse their power, labour relations boards declare it an unfair labour practice for employers to communicate with their employees about unionization at the time certification proceedings are underway. Again the majority of both unionized and non-unionized workers in our survey disagree with this ban (#11).

Since re-election in 1983 leaders of the British Columbia Social Credit government have legislated some restrictions on union powers, and talked of more drastic measures yet to come. The most significant of their 1984 legislative amendments was elimination of the ability of unions to obtain certification of a new bargaining unit on the basis that a majority of workers in the unit had signed union cards. Henceforth certification requires two steps: first, the union sign up a required percentage of workers and, second, a majority of all workers vote for union certification in a subsequent election organized by the provincial Labour Relations Board. Elections prior to certification is the American practice. Canadian union leaders have traditionally opposed it as an unjustifiable increase in the costs of organizing, and as a delay that increases the potential for employers to intimidate workers in support of a union. Social Credit politicians argue that past practice made it too easy for union organizers to intimidate, that a secret ballot assures a more democratic result. Our survey results suggest that a large majority of both union and non-union workers accept the government's position (#13).

Recent legislative changes in British Columbia have also made secondary picketing more restrictive and decertification of a union by dissatisfied union members somewhat easier. In our sample a majority of workers, whether unionized or not, oppose secondary picketing in principle and think decertification currently too difficult (#14, #15).

Actual vs. Desired Influence over Decisions

A conservative would interpret results in the previous section to mean that a majority of workers oppose in principle many of the powers currently exercised by unions to restrict employer access to non-union labour and thereby increase union wages. The conservative may in part be right. But he would be wrong if he sought to generalize that workers accept the inherent logic of capitalism in which managers, as agents of owners, give the orders, and workers obey. On the contrary, workers want more influence over decisions at work than the typical private firm or public bureaucracy allows.

Using the methodology of a survey of British workers,[4] we posed a series of questions to compare desired and actual levels of influence over management decisions (#20—#25). These questions were posed only to those who are currently working for a wage or salary, or who have done so in the last five years. We divided decisions into three categories: personal decisions (e.g. hours of work, job duties, holiday scheduling), administrative decisions (e.g. hiring and firing, selection of supervisors) and major policy decisions (e.g. financial investment and planning, introduction of new technology). For each category of decision we invited respondents to describe their own situation by choosing from a continuum: "no influence" (1), "a little influence" (2), "a lot of influence" (3), "complete control" (4).

Do workers want more influence than they actually have? Using the indicated numbers, we calculated average responses. The higher the average, the higher is the level of influence, actual or desired, for the group. While the average response provides a useful summary of results, the reader should be aware of the limitations. We are assuming that the responses mean the same thing to all those sampled, and that it makes sense to assign numbers to responses, thereby inventing "units of influence". Is the difference between a little influence and no influence the same as that between a lot and a little? By our interpretation yes; both equal one "unit". Here we restrict our consideration to the average responses calculated. The reader can examine the appendix for the distribution of results by specific scale responses. The first observation is that, for each of the three categories, workers want more influence than they actually have—about half a unit more. For example, the actual level of influence over personal decisions among all workers is 2.27, somewhat more than "a little"; the desired level of influence over personal decisions, at 2.80, is close to "a lot of influence". We might refer to the difference between desired and actual influence as the "degree of frustration". While workers predictably want more influence over personal than administrative decisions, more over administrative than major policy decisions, it is interesting to note that the degree of frustration is approximately the same for all three categories of decisions.

These questions contain some other interesting results. Unionized workers perceive themselves exercising less influence than non-unionized workers. In response to questions about desired level of influence unionized workers also want somewhat less influence than the non-unionized, but the union-non-union gap has narrowed. In other words the degree of frustration of unionized workers is higher. Access to collective bargaining on the part of unionized workers may have lowered their frustration relative to what it would otherwise have been, but it remains above that for the non-unionized. The non-unionized comprises a very diverse group A similar argument applies to women relative to men. Women perceive themselves exercising less influence over all categories of decisions than do men. They also want somewhat less influence, but the gap has narrowed. So the degree of frustration as measured is higher for women than for men.

Labour participation in management

Collective bargaining is one means, and a valuable means, whereby workers can collectively exercise influence in the making of decisions at their place of work. It is not, however, the only means. We posed a series of questions on codetermination as a supplementary means. A large majority of the sample obviously support the idea. Our results are consistent with results on worker participation elicited by Decima in a 1983 nation-wide study.[5]

Before posing the question on support, we introduced several of the standard arguments raised for and against codetermination. One economic argument in favour is that workers can obtain more and better information about their firm, which enables them to take a more entrepreneurial perspective, considering the long run implications for the firm of their demands. A second argument in favour is that codetermination requires managers to pay more attention to the implications on their workers of management decisions. To the extent both workers and capitalists can benefit from making efficient decisions, codetermination should benefit all concerned. Our respondents overwhelmingly think codetermination would increase workers' access to relevant information about their firms, and that this would increase efficiency (#26). Overwhelmingly they also think firms "would operate better because managers would take workers' interests more into account" (#28).

A conservative counterargument suggests that workers have no interest in efficiency and that the presence of their representatives in the board room would block the ability of managers to make efficient decisions, would lower firm profits and, ultimately, workers' wages. A large majority of respondents reject this argument (#27). Finally, some left wing critics of codetermination fear it as a form of "class collaboration" that will sap worker commitment to collective bargaining for maximum wages. As with the right wing objection, this argument is rejected by a large majority of the sample (#29). Significantly, it is also rejected to the same extent by union workers.

Overall nearly five out of six in the sample think workers on the boards of large companies would be a "good thing" (#30). This result is somewhat higher than the result obtained by Gallup in 1977 in a national survey using a question with the same wording.[6] Surprisingly, agreement on this idea extends fairly uniformly across supporters of the different political parties. Division of the sample according to the electoral choices in either the 1983 provincial or 1984 federal elections produces only minor variations. Predictably supporters of the Conservatives and Social Credit favour the idea somewhat less than supporters of the NDP or Liberals, but the differences are not large. Female workers favour the idea somewhat more than male workers; unionized workers somewhat more than the non-unionized.

An important supplementary question to pose is the degree of participation in board level decision-making that people want workers to exercise. To those who thought codetermination a "good thing" we asked their opinion on the appropriate proportion of directors workers should elect (#31). Do they want worker board representatives restricted to a nominal proportion? Do they want parity (as one of us argues in Chapter V) to be optimum? What support exists for the radical idea that workers dominate, and be able to elect a majority of board members? Overall, and for all identifiable subgroups, the most frequently chosen option is to grant workers one third of board members. Three in ten want only nominal worker representation of less than ten percent; one in four want workers to achieve parity or majority status. Predictably, a higher proportion of Social Credit and Conservative supporters want nominal worker representation than do supporters of the NDP.

This last question shows that four out of seven respondents favour workers obtaining at least a third of board positions. This is the fraction prevalent in codetermination laws of a number of European countries.

---

[1] The authors designed the questionnaire and supervised the survey, as a project in a Canadian Studies seminar we jointly offered. Interviews were conducted by our students in the seminar: Liz Bell, Fred Berenbaum, Vic Farmer, Ian Foster, David Fraser, Peter Godman, Robert Langmaid, Frank Parker, Anne-Marie Sleeman, and Paul Wilson. Without their work the survey could not have been undertaken. We gratefully acknowledge their many hours in revising the questionnaire and in telephoning.

[2] Here are three references on the (mis)use of polls: G. Gallup, *The Sophisticated Poll Watcher's Guide* (Princeton: Princeton Opinion Press, 1972); H.L. Nieburg, *Public Opinion, Tracking and Targeting* (New York: Praeger, 1984); C.W. Roll jr. & A.H. Cantril, *Polls, their Use and Misuse in Politics* (New York: Basic Books, 1972).

[3] *The Decima Quarterly Report*, quarterly (Toronto: Decima Research Ltd.).

[4] F. Heller et al., *What do the British Want from Participation and Industrial Democracy?* (London: Anglo-German Foundation for the Study of Industrial Society, 1979).

[5] See "In-depth Analysis: Changing Patterns in the Work Place", *The Decima Quarterly Report*, IV, 2 (Summer 1983). In this study 65% agreed (25% disagreed) with the statement, "I would like to take a more active

part in the decisions which affect the future of the company I work for''. In addition to the above question on personal involvement, Decima also posed a question on union participation in corporate management. Here they asked respondents to choose between two statements: "Some people say that companies would run better if unions had representatives on the company's board of directors. Other people say that unions are there to look after employees and that it's up to the managers to run the company. Thinking of these two points of view, which one best reflects your own?" Relative to the item on personal involvement, support for worker participation was lower. Overall, 42% favoured the first statement; 56% the second.

⁶"7-in-10 Approve Worker Reps on Board of Directors," *The Gallup Report* (Toronto: The Canadian Institute of Public Opinion, 1977).

Questionnaire and Summary Results

I'd like to begin with some general questions. I'm going to name some institutions in this country and I'd like you to consider the people who run these institutions.

1   How about the people who run multinational corporations? Would you say you have a great deal of confidence in them, only some confidence in them, or hardly any confidence in them?

	a great deal	only some	hardly any	don't know
total (of sample)	20%	57%	17%	6%
union (workers)	19%	58%	20%	4%
non-union (workers)	20%	59%	13%	8%

2   How about the people who run unions? Would you say you have a great deal of confidence in them, only some confidence, or hardly any confidence?

	a great deal	only some	hardly any	don't know
total	10%	43%	44%	3%
union	17%	47%	35%	1%
non-union	7%	41%	48%	5%
provincial vote, 1983				
NDP	15%	58%	24%	3%
Social Credit	7%	41%	49%	2%
federal vote, 1984				
Conservative	5%	37%	56%	2%
Liberal	10%	45%	40%	5%
NDP	13%	71%	13%	3%

3   How about the people who run the banks? Would you say you have a
great deal of confidence in them, only some confidence, or hardly
any confidence?

	a great deal	only some	hardly any	don't know
total	25%	54%	20%	2%
union	28%	54%	17%	2%
non-union	20%	55%	23%	2%

*I'm going to read some statements. For each would you say if you strongly agree,
mildly agree, mildly disagree, or strongly disagree? (Results have been aggregated in
these tables.)*

4   The growth of unionism has made our democracy stronger.

	agree	disagree	don't know
total	59%	40%	2%
union	66%	33%	1%
non-union	55%	43%	2%

5   Union demands often contribute to unemployment.

	agree	disagree	don't know
total	64%	34%	2%
union	54%	45%	1%
non-union	68%	30%	2%
provincial NDP	47%	52%	1%
federal NDP	46%	53%	2%

6   When it comes to determining wages and working conditions, the
employers' power needs to be balanced by unions.

	agree	disagree	don't know
total	71%	29%	1%
union	81%	20%	0%
non-union	65%	32%	1%

7   Union leaders usually represent the best interests of their members.

	agree	disagree	don't know
total	44%	55%	1%
union	56%	43%	1%
non-union	37%	63%	1%

8   Every worker should be free to decide whether or not to join the union where he works.

	agree	disagree	don't know
total	89%	11%	1%
union	82%	19%	0%
non-union	91%	8%	1%

9   In a case of layoffs the best person should be kept on the job regardless of seniority.

	agree	disagree	don't know
total	71%	24%	5%
union	66%	32%	2%
non-union	76%	19%	6%

10.   Without unions workers would have little protection against favouritism by management.

	agree	disagree	don't know
total	66%	32%	2%
union	79%	20%	1%
non-union	58%	39%	3%

11   Employers should have a say in the decision by their workers to unionize.

	agree	disagree	don't know
total	61%	37%	3%
union	57%	39%	4%
non-union	65%	34%	1%

I'd like to turn to some issues concerning the labour code. Governments have created collective bargaining legislation, known as the labour code, to regulate the operation of unions. There has been discussion recently in British Columbia about changes to this legislation. I'd appreciate your opinion on the subject.

12   Which of the following two statements better corresponds to your view?

A. *Without* the labour code, workers would be at a disadvantage in bargaining with employers over wages and terms of work, or

B. *With* the labour code, there is too much interference with the rights of individual workers and employers to do what they want.

	A	B	don't know
total	57%	31%	12%
union	67%	28%	5%
non-union	52%	30%	19%

13   In general which of the following two statements better corresponds to your views about the certification of unions?

A. The government should automatically allow certification if a majority of a group of workers sign forms saying they want a union, or

B. Before certifying, the government should organize an election with a secret ballot among the workers to decide if they want a union.

Keep in mind that some people think formal elections give management the chance to intimidate workers, while others think that, without an election, it is too easy for union organizers to intimidate workers.

	A	B	don't know
total	14%	82%	5%
union	24%	75%	1%
non-union	10%	85%	5%

For each of the following statements do you strongly agree, mildly agree, mildly disagree, or strongly disagree? (Results have been aggregated in these tables.)

14 During strikes and lockouts union members should be allowed to
    picket sites other than their own place of work.

	agree	disagree	don't know
total	26%	73%	2%
union	35%	65%	0%
non-union	21%	77%	3%

15 At present, it is too difficult for unionized workers to get rid of their
    union if the majority don't want it.

	agree	disagree	don't know
total	75%	16%	9%
union	69%	24%	7%
non-union	79%	11%	11%

16 In general public sector workers—such as teachers, bus driv-
    ers and civil servants—should continue to have the right to
    strike.

	agree	disagree	don't know
total	60%	38%	2%
union	77%	23%	0%
non-union	54%	43%	4%

17 Public sector workers in essential services—such as policing, fire-
    fighting, and nursing—should continue to have at least a limited
    right to strike.

	agree	disagree	don't know
total	56%	42%	2%
union	69%	31%	0%
non-union	54%	43%	3%

18 The government should be more willing to legislate an end to strikes and lockouts that cost the economy a great deal.

	agree	disagree	don't know
total	75%	18%	2%
union	69%	29%	2%
non-union	84%	15%	1%

19 Are you currently working outside the home for a wage or salary, or have you done so in the last five years? (Questions #20—#25 were posed only to those who answered "yes".)

	yes	no
total	78%	22%

20 At work, how much influence do you *actually* have over *personal* decisions such as hours of work, job duties, holiday time? Which of the following best applies to you: no influence, a little influence, a lot of influence, complete control? (See text for interpretation of "average response".)

	average response	no influence	a little influence	a lot of influence	complete control
total	2.27	24%	39%	25%	13%
union	2.07	23%	54%	16%	7%
non-union	2.39	24%	29%	31%	16%
male	2.38	22%	34%	27%	16%
female	2.11	25%	45%	24%	6%

21 How much influence would you *like* to have over *personal* decisions?

	average response	no influence	a little influence	a lot of influence	complete control
total	2.80	4%	29%	50%	17%
union	2.73	2%	36%	50%	13%
non-union	2.85	5%	25%	50%	20%
male	2.87	4%	27%	49%	21%
female	2.69	5%	32%	52%	11%

22   At work, how much influence do you *actually* have over *administrative* decisions such as hiring and firing, choice of supervisors, job training programs?

	average response	no influence	a little influence	a lot of influence	complete control
total	1.86	49%	27%	14%	11%
union	1.59	59%	27%	8%	5%
non-union	2.03	42%	27%	17%	15%
male	1.95	45%	29%	11%	15%
female	1.72	54%	24%	17%	5%

23   How much influence would you *like* to have over *administrative* decisions?

	average response	no influence	a little influence	a lot of influence	complete control
total	2.39	16%	43%	28%	13%
union	2.18	19%	51%	24%	6%
non-union	2.52	14%	39%	30%	18%
male	2.44	15%	42%	28%	15%
female	2.28	18%	45%	28%	9%

24   At work, how much influence do you *actually* have over *major policy* decisions such as financial investment and planning, introduction of new equipment?

	average response	no influence	a little influence	a lot of influence	complete control
total	1.66	58%	27%	7%	8%
union	1.39	69%	25%	4%	2%
non-union	1.83	51%	28%	10%	12%
male	1.78	51%	31%	7%	11%
female	1.50	67%	21%	7%	5%

25   How much influence would you *like* to have over *major policy* decisions?

	average response	no influence	a little influence	a lot of influence	complete control
total	2.22	21%	45%	25%	9%
union	2.08	22%	51%	24%	3%
non-union	2.32	19%	42%	26%	13%
male	2.31	20%	42%	25%	13%
female	2.11	20%	52%	23%	4%

Today, workers have some influence on decision-making through unions and collective bargaining. Recently, some have proposed that workers also elect representatives to company boards of directors. I'm going to read four statements about this idea. For each would you say whether you strongly agree, mildly agree, mildly disagree, strongly disagree. (Results have been aggregated in these tables.)

26   The company would operate more efficiently because workers would be better informed about the company.

	agree	disagree	don't know
total	90%	9%	1%
union	94%	4%	2%
non-union	90%	9%	1%

27   The company would be less profitable because the worker representatives would prevent managers from making efficient decisions.

	agree	disagree	don't know
total	22%	75%	3%
union	20%	78%	2%
non-union	21%	78%	2%

28 The company would operate better because managers would take workers' interests more into account.

	agree	disagree	don't know
total	83%	15%	2%
union	87%	11%	2%
non-union	85%	14%	1%

29 Having worker directors would weaken the willingness of workers to bargain hard for wage increases, and this would make workers worse off.

	agree	disagree	don't know
total	15%	79%	7%
union	13%	79%	7%
non-union	14%	81%	5%

30 In general do you think it would be a good thing or a bad thing if workers in large companies were able to elect members on the board of directors?

	good thing	bad thing	don't know
total	82%	15%	4%
union	88%	9%	3%
non-union	79%	18%	3%
male	78%	19%	2%
female	86%	10%	5%
provincial vote, 1983			
NDP	88%	11%	1%
Social Credit	83%	16%	1%
federal vote, 1984			
Conservative	80%	15%	5%
Liberal	90%	8%	3%
NDP	90%	10%	0%

31   What proportion of directors do you think workers should be able
to elect? (This question was posed to those answering "good
thing" to #30.)

	under 10%	a third	a half	a majority	don't know
total	29%	46%	18%	6%	2%
union	29%	44%	17%	10%	1%
non-union	30%	47%	16%	6%	2%
male	32%	47%	16%	4%	2%
female	26%	45%	20%	8%	2%
● provincial vote 1983					
NDP	27%	48%	15%	7%	3%
Social Credit	36%	40%	19%	4%	0%
● federal vote 1984					
Conservative	32%	48%	15%	4%	0%
Liberal	28%	43%	20%	3%	5%
NDP	17%	57%	15%	9%	2%

Industrial Democracy: Some Practical Observations

Don Ching

This is not an academic analysis of industrial relations or worker participation in the work place. Rather, it is one person's view of an industrial democracy experiment—in a Saskatchewan crown corporation—and a few observations from one who believes that the next major step towards social democracy in Canada must be to bring democracy to the work place.[1]

Led by Allan Blakeney the Saskatchewan NDP was first elected in 1971. The election was greeted by most working people with great enthusiasm. Both rank-and-file workers and their union representatives had major expectations of the new government. Reforms of the Trade Union Act and of the Labour Standards Act, and enactment of a new Occupational Health Act satisfied some of these expectations. The new occupational health program gave legislative responsibility for occupational health matters to joint labour-management committees required by law to be established in firms above a minimum size. It was a step towards greater industrial democracy. However by 1975 crown corporation and government employees were restive that the government was making no moves to change the traditional relationship between itself as employer and its employees. Government employees felt that a worker-oriented government should be different from a private employer, but they began to feel there was no really significant difference.

Government leaders were conscious of this restiveness and at the political level there was a general but ill-defined wish to investigate and experiment with new management structures—such as those implemented by certain European social democractic governments—that would address the problem. In government and the labour movement there was a flirtation with the idea of industrial democracy. A number of us in government or associated with the newly created Potash Corporation of Saskatchewan (PCS) concluded that the potash takeover presented a unique opportunity to experiment with increased employee participation in management. To understand the experiment at PCS it helps to know a little of the history of the corporation.

The Potash Corporation of Saskatchewan

From the beginning in 1971 the new cabinet wanted to further public involvement in the natural resource sector and to extract greater revenue for the public purse. (See Chapter III for the perspective of Elwood Cowley who for much of the NDP's time in office was the minister responsible for mineral resources.) By the end of the government's first term it had instituted important new taxes on the potash industry and established an embryonic crown-owned potash corporation, PCS. These initiatives alarmed and antagonized industry management which retaliated by withholding taxes and financial information from the government. The dispute simmered through the spring of 1975. After re-election of the NDP in a general election in the summer of that year most producers jointly launched a lawsuit challenging the constitutional authority of the government's initiatives.

In response the cabinet announced in November, 1975, at the opening of the new legislature, that the government intended to acquire all or a significant portion of the Saskatchewan potash industry, and to operate it through PCS. Between November, 1975 and March, 1978 the government acquired four producing potash mines. (It also acquired a portion of the output of a fifth for which it undertook no operational responsibilities.) These four mines—strung out in a straight line from Saskatoon east to the Manitoba border—are conventional shaft mines with an underground operation to harvest the potash ore, and a surface operation to refine, store and ship the finished product, potassium chloride, virtually all of which is used as agricultural fertilizer.

Hourly paid workers at two of the PCS mines were represented by the United Steelworkers of America. As well, first line supervisors at one of these mines were organized in a separate Steelworkers local. Hourly workers at a third PCS mine were represented by the Energy and Chemical Workers. Initially not unionized, hourly workers at the fourth mine established shortly after government acquisition an independent employee's association, and it became certified as their bargaining representative.

While some trade union leaders were both knowledgeable about and interested in industrial democracy, the majority of the union movement vacillated between ambivalence and outright hostility towards the idea. In PCS union suspicions were exacerbated by the existence of three separate unions. In the province of Saskatchewan the Steelworkers and Energy and

Chemical Workers have a history of competition for the right to represent workers in mining companies. This competition tainted the view of leaders of both these unions to overtures from PCS management to experiment with industrial democracy. Further, neither union viewed the employee's association at the fourth mine to be a legitimate representative of unionized employees. Both suspected managers within PCS, especially those located at the fourth mine site, of having encouraged formation of the association to keep out a "real" union.

Despite these impediments PCS possessed some important advantages as the setting for an industrial democracy experiment. First, each of the acquired mines was successfully operational, and such an experiment would not be hampered by the peculiar start-up needs of a major enterprise. Second, the period after crown acquisition was one of controlled turbulence which could prove fertile for innovation. While each mine retained almost all the former private managers and very few of these managers were sympathetic to the idea of worker participation, they realized this was a time of change. Their level of resistance to change was probably as low as one could reasonably expect to find at an operating mine site. Third, the leaders of the unions representing potash miners, the new senior managers at PCS, and senior government leaders were well known to each other. Despite a general suspicion among union leaders towards industrial democracy both the Steelworkers and the Energy and Chemical Workers had actively campaigned for government takeover of potash, and had a vested interest in the success of PCS. Both unions had a history of strong but responsible representation of their members.

Industrial democracy and PCS

How does one start to expose a major crown corporation to industrial democracy? At the time, in 1978, I was a vice-president of PCS with responsibility for, amongst other things, industrial relations at the four mine sites. The vice-president responsible for mine operations and I were jointly responsible for the actual takeover of mine administration after acquisition. In conjunction with the Director of Industrial Relations we set up the "Industrial Democracy Study Group". A loosely structured organization, it included head office managers, local mine managers, staff representatives of the individual unions and the elected presidents of the union locals. The three of us who launched the study group wanted it to explore different concepts of industrial democracy, look at industrial relations in other countries and to see how PCS structures could be altered to enhance employee decision-making. The study group began to meet in the spring of 1978 upon completion of mine acquisitions.

Meetings of the study group were an unofficial gathering for a cross-section of those who made up PCS, ranging from vice-presidents to a hoist operator. Typical meetings began with a speaker on some aspect of industrial democracy. Afterwards we conducted extensive discussions that often continued over supper. We examined reports from organizations such as the International Labour Organization (ILO), and members brought forward diverse articles on industrial relations. We discussed many ideas: how to expand the flow of information about the actual performance of PCS from management to union and to rank-and-file workers, whether it was desirable for employees to elect members to the company board of directors, how to assure that industrial democracy innovations not interfere with the rights of workers to conduct collective bargaining, to what extent first and second level supervision could be undertaken by workers themselves.

A subgroup was struck to visit other jurisdictions experimenting with industrial democracy. Like the study group itself, this subgroup comprised a cross-section of people at PCS. In the fall of 1978 the subgroup visited Yugoslavia, West Germany and Sweden, spending a week in each country. Initially in each country Canadian embassy officials and experts on domestic industrial relations briefed us. Thereafter we visited employment sites—to observe, to meet representatives of management and workers and to discuss in depth their individual operations. As well, we met representatives of trade unions, of employer organizations and of the host governments. Much of the value of this activity was to bring together people representing a cross-section of PCS, to spend extended time together under circumstances where they were continually bombarded by discussions about industrial relations. One of the subgroup recommendations upon its return was, incidentally, the desirability that out-of-scope employees do as in Sweden—organize collective associations to argue their particular interests within PCS.

In early 1979 the industrial democracy experiment underwent a major transformation, becoming more formally organized but less ambitious in scope. At the time I and the other vice-president who had instigated the experiment ceased our active involvement. The remaining members of the study group decided to transform it into the "Work Environment Board", a joint labour-management committee within PCS, chaired by an external person, the then Assistant Deputy Minister of Labour who also headed the occupational health and safety division. This new Work Environment Board was more formally structured than the old study group, and received a substantial budget allocation from PCS. The interest of this new group was more modestly directed towards occupational health than towards global changes in the managerial structure of PCS. It was understood however that occupational health is simply one aspect of industrial democracy.

While tracing their origins is difficult, some innovations in collective bargaining at PCS evolved from these dialogues on industrial democracy. At least two of the collective bargaining agreements subsequently negotiated contained clauses allowing individual employees a hearing before a joint meeting (of the mine manager and local union president) before discipline could be meted out. This is a small but significant example of a change in attitude on responsibility for discipline. Another example was that PCS agreed at each mine to release a specified number of man-years of employee time at full salary to do union work. This was seen as a preliminary step to turning over some functions to worker representatives. Among these functions was scheduling of holidays, scheduling of shifts, handling of layoffs and recalls. A third innovation was establishment of an employee recovery program funded by the employer and jointly controlled by union and management. It provided assistance to any employee suffering from alcoholism or drug abuse, family breakdown or similar problems.

Some observations on industrial democracy

In the general election held in April, 1982 the provincial Conservatives defeated the NDP. By that summer numerous senior PCS managers, including the president, had been forced out. The Work Environment Board passed into history and with it this experiment in industrial democracy.

Were the gains made worth all the effort put into it, and the depression experienced when the modest gains were rolled back? My answer is yes. Clearly the union representatives involved, and many of their members, came to look upon the experiment with enthusiasm and hope. The unions had entered the process with much scepticism, but they rapidly realized it was a legitimate effort to analyze changes that could better individual employees. Even if subsequent events have again raised suspicions among trade unionists about industrial democracy, the experiment has not left them unchanged. They are aware of the potential which would arise from a long-term effort with sustained support from management and unions. Similarly, while many of the advocates of industrial democracy have left PCS management, the ideas of those who remain have changed somewhat.

Nonetheless significant difficulties were apparent from the beginning in the industrial democracy experiment. First, no one, including the instigators of the experiment among senior PCS management, had a clear blueprint of accomplishments for the experiment. Senior government leaders had only the vaguest of ideas about industrial democracy. While their support for the idea in abstract was readily forthcoming, support for implementation of industrial democracy proposals was not. For example, the government displayed in general outright hostility to the idea of crown corporation employees as members of corporation boards of directors.

Second, both government leaders and senior PCS managers had an overpowering desire that PCS be financially successful and managerially well-run in a traditional private enterprise manner. Given that PCS had been spawned in controversy, NDP politicians were anxious to show to the public that the government could successfully operate a major crown corporation in a resource industry. Strangely, government leaders could see these political consequences, but failed to see the political consequences of treating its employees—who also happen to be voters—in the same manner as do privately owned companies. It is a trite observation, but few owners or senior corporate executives could be democratically elected to their positions by their own employees. In both publicly and privately owned companies, in Saskatchewan as elsewhere, employees feel manipulated by the owners and executives, and feel alienated from the decision-making of their enterprises. Despite this obvious fact government politicians, the "owners" of crown corporations, who must seek re-election from not only the general electorate but their own employees, persist in operating publicly owned corporations in the same manner as privately owned firms.

Third, it was a major failing of the industrial democracy experiment not to take into account the interests of junior and middle management.

Essentially the experiment embraced head office and senior mine site managers, union hired staff and elected representatives. While the employee representatives enjoyed a degree of support from their constituents, and reported to workers on the experiment, no such accounting occurred between the management representatives and their constituency, junior and middle management. The managers did not perceive themselves representing other managers; they were present in their personal capacities. As a result many managers, especially at the first and second level, were largely unaware of the experiment, and to the extent they were aware, they were suspicious of it. Perhaps given more time their suspicions would have been addressed. During the experiment however they were not addressed, despite the fact that worker participation in management would seriously affect the operation—and perhaps the very existence—of first and second level supervisors.

Two general conclusions are worth stating. Clearly any experimentation in industrial democracy will have to balance the need of corporations—both privately and publicly owned—to maximize the return on their financial investment with the need of individual employees to participate in the control of their work day lives. Creative corporate structures must respond to both needs.

Finally, while union leaders and individual workers at PCS felt a loss when the industrial democracy experiment collapsed in 1982, there was insufficient understanding of its potential to create a strong worker demand that it continue. A substantial organizational effort has to be made among working people to encourage them to think that they do indeed have the right and the responsibility to control their work lives, as they control their non-work lives. To date the industrial democracy debate has been largely restricted to the academic arena, and to a few experiments such as that at PCS. It is time to expand the debate. The New Democratic Party, with its many ties to organized labour, is ideally placed to act as catalyst for a wide debate on industrial democracy— among workers, union leaders and even corporate managers.

---

[1] I want to thank Roy Romanow and John Richards for comments on earlier drafts of this essay.

Appendices

Biographies of Participants

Don Aitken is Secretary Treasurer of the Alberta Federation of Labour and has been General Services Director of that organization for six years. He is currently a member of the Board of Directors of the Alberta Council on Aging and was founding co-ordinator of the Alberta Friends of Medicare. As well, he is a former president of the Alberta NDP and serves as an executive member of the federal NDP.

Allan Blakeney was born in Nova Scotia, graduated from Dalhousie University in law and studied economics and political science at Oxford University as a Rhodes Scholar. He has served in the Saskatchewan legislature for 25 years. In the last CCF government between 1960 and 1964 he held several portfolios: Education, Health and Treasury. He became leader of the Saskatchewan NDP in 1970, served as Premier of the province from 1971 to 1982 and now leads the Opposition in the Legislature.

Gerald Caplan joined the CCF in 1957 and has remained a party activist since. He has a MA in Canadian history and a PhD in African history and was for ten years a university teacher specializing in third world underdevelopment and Canadian political culture. He was a founding member of the Waffle prior to the 1969 federal NDP convention, but left it to become campaign manager for Ontario NDP leader Stephen Lewis, a job he performed in all three of Lewis' provincial election campaigns. After Lewis' resignation as provincial leader, Caplan spent two years as director of the CUSO program in Nigeria, directed an experiment in public health for the Health Advocacy Unit in Toronto, became NDP federal secretary and was federal campaign manager for the NDP in the 1984 election. He is now co-chair of the federal government's Task Force on Broadcast Policy.

Donald Ching was born at Oxbow, Saskatchewan in 1941. He received a BA and LLB in 1967 and an Honours Degree in Far Eastern Studies in 1971, all from the University of Saskatchewan in Saskatoon. He practised law from 1967 until election of the Saskatchewan NDP in 1971. From 1971 to 1974 he was Deputy Minister of the provincial

Labour Department. For a year he headed the government agency responsible for provincial crown corporations, and then for three years was Executive Vice-President of the Potash Corporation of Saskatchewan, a provincial crown corporation. In 1979 he set up his own law practice, specializing in labour law, and began lecturing in industrial relations at the University of Saskatchewan. He is presently a senior partner in the Saskatoon law firm of Mitchell, Taylor, Romanow & Ching.

Elwood Cowley was born in Saskatoon in 1944 and was active in the CCF youth movement. He was first elected to the Saskatchewan legislature in 1971, was re-elected in 1975 and 1978, and defeated in the 1982 Conservative landslide. He served in the NDP cabinet as Minister of Finance, Minister of Economic Development and Minister of the Crown Investment Corporation.

Sam Gindin is Research Director for the Canadian United Auto Workers, a position he has held since 1974. He was raised in Winnipeg, received a BA from the University of Manitoba and a MA in economics from the University of Wisconsin in Madison.

Tom Gunton was born in Burlington, Ontario and he obtained his first degree from the University of Waterloo. He received a PhD in planning from the University of British Columbia. He currently teaches resource policy and economic development at Simon Fraser University, and since 1982 has worked as advisor to the Government of Manitoba. He was chairman of the Economic Policy Committee of the British Columbia NDP from 1976 to 1981.

Don Kerr was born in Saskatoon in 1936 and teaches English at the University of Saskatchewan. He has co-written a history of Saskatoon, edited *Western Canadian Politics: the Radical Tradition* (1981), and co-edited a collection of prairie plays in the populist tradition, *Showing West* (1982), and is a poet and playwright. He was involved in John Richards' two election campaigns in Saskatoon in the first half of the 1970s, and in the attempt to bring co-operatively controlled cable television to Saskatchewan in the second half of the 70s.

Arthur Kube was born in Poland, moved with his family to Austria and then emigrated to Canada in 1949. He worked in mining and steel fabrication industries, became active as an organizer and was five times fired for union activities. In 1961 he was appointed to the staff of the Canadian Labour Congress and stationed in Sudbury. In 1969 he organized the White Collar organizing program for the CLC, and in 1974 was appointed Regional Director of Education for British Columbia. In 1983 he was elected president of the British Columbia Federation of Labour and was centrally involved in the Solidarity campaign that year against the provincial government's "restraint" program. He is currently a member of the CLC Executive Council.

Norman MacLellan was born in The Pas, Manitoba, lived and worked in British Columbia from 1962 to 1977 and became a union activist in 1965. He is at present the national representative for the Canadian Paperworkers Union respnsible for Alberta and Saskatchewan, an Alberta Federation of Labour Vice-President and Vice-President of the Representative and Organizers Union. He was president of the Mackenzie NDP constituency association in British Columbia between 1973 and 1974.

Patricia Marchak is a professor in the Department of Anthropology and Sociology at the University of British Columbia and author of three books: *Ideological Perspectives on Canada* (1975), *In Whose Interests: Multinational Corporations in a Canadian Context* (1979), *Green Gold: the Forest Industry in British Columbia* (1983). She is a past president of the Canadian Sociology and Anthropology Association, and is currently doing research on forestry and fisheries in British Columbia. She was an unsuccessful candidate running for the NDP in a Vancouver riding in the 1983 provincial election.

Gary Mauser teaches at Simon Fraser University in Vancouver, specializing in survey research and voter behaviour. He received his PhD from the University of California at Irvine. He has been active in the British Columbia NDP, and has advised the party on polling, campaign strategy and use of computers.

Grant Notley was born in 1939 in Olds, Alberta, received a BA from the University of Alberta and became interested at university in the campus CCF. In 1962 he became provincial secretary of the NDP and in 1968 party leader. He was first elected to the legislature in 1971, and three times re-elected by the voters of his Spirit River-Fairview constituency in the Peace River area. He died in October, 1984.

Leo Panitch was born in North Winnipeg in 1945, educated at the University of Manitoba and the London School of Ecnomics. He taught political science for twelve years at Carleton University in Ottawa and is now at York University in Toronto. He has published three books: *Social Democracy and Industrial Militancy: the Labour Party, the Trade Unions and Incomes Policy* (1976), *The Canadian State: Political Economy and Political Power* (1977), *From Consent to Coercion: the Assault on Trade Union Freedoms* (1985). A collection of his essays will be forthcoming this year: *Working Class Politics in Crisis: Essays on Labour and the State*. He is an editor on the journal *Studies in Political Economy*, and was a founding member and activist in the Ottawa Committee for Labour Action.

John Richards was born in England in 1944, but emigrated to Saskatchewan where he received his first degree. He also studied at Cambridge University, England, and Washington University, St. Louis, USA. In the United States in the late 1960s he was active in political campaigns against the Vietnam War. In 1970 he returned to Saskatoon and taught for a year at the University of Saskatchewan. He served as a member of the Saskatchewan legislature between 1971 and 1975, for the first two years as legislative secretary to the Minister of Health, for the last two years in the opposition. In 1975 he ran unsuccessfully for re-election as an "independent socialist". He has since mellowed and rejoined the NDP. With Larry Pratt he co-authored *Prairie Capitalism* (1979), and currently teaches at Simon Fraser University. As president since 1982 of the board of REACH, a Vancouver community health centre, he has had some practical experience in trying to make industrial democracy work.

Jim Russell was born in Montreal to parents from the Maritimes and largely grew up in Quebec City during the days of Duplessis' regime. The family were members of the League for Social Reconstruction in the 1930s. He studied chemistry at Dalhousie, at the university of Saskatchewan, where he received his PhD, and at Leeds University,

England, before returning to the University of Alberta in 1964. There he took up an appointment in the Department of Surgery in 1967. The rise of the Committee for an Independent Canada in the early 1970s brought him into active political life, and he was intimately involved in policy creation, especially on energy. In the mid-1970s he became active in the Alberta NDP and has been Chairman of the Energy and Economic Development Policy Committees. After considerable arm twisting by Grant Notley and Ray Martin, he was a candidate in the 1979 and 1982 provincial elections.

Richard Schwindt was born in San Francisco in 1944. He did both his undergraduate and graduate work at the University of California at Berkeley, surviving the Free Speech Movement, the Anti-War Movement and the reign of Ronald Reagan as governor of California. He took an academic appointment at Simon Fraser University in 1972 and has been there ever since. He is an economist by training and persuasion. He specializes in industrial economics and the regulation of industry, particularly anti-combines policy. He has researched the industrial organization of renewable resource industries such as the Pacific fisheries and forestry, and he has also published on the industrial economics of Canadian banking and tourism. As well, he has consulted for the federal Bureau of Competition Policy on a number of anti-combines cases. Most recently he assisted the government on its case against major oil companies before the Restrictive Trade Practices Committee's Petroleum Inquiry.

Garth Stevenson is professor of political science at the University of Alberta, where he has taught since 1978. He was previously on the faculty of Carleton University. He is the author of *Unfulfilled Union: Canadian Federalism and National Unity* (1979), and co-author with Larry Pratt of *Western Separatism: the Myths, Realilties and Dangers* (1981). He compiled the "Federalism" section of *The New Practical Guide to Canadian Political Economy* (1978), edited by Daniel Drache and Wallace Clement, and has just completed a book on air transport policy in Canada. He has written extensively on Australian as well as Canadian federalism. Stevenson was a constitutional advisor to the Alberta NDP in 1980-81. He has been a NDP candidate for the Ontario legislature in 1971, the Alberta legislature in 1982, and the House of Commons in 1984.

Davis Swan was born at Beaver Lake, near Sudbury, Ontario, the son of an INCO miner and an elementary school teacher. He received a BA from the University of Guelph and a BSc from the University of British Columbia. He worked for the Geological Survey of Canada before joining Gulf Oil as a staff geophysicist. Between 1978 and 1983 he was a member of the executive of the Alberta NDP, and ran as a provincial candidate in 1982. Since 1980 he has been energy critic for the Alberta NDP. He worked closely with Grant Notley on energy and economic policy, and was among those who developed the *June 22nd Statement of Principles* prior to the 1983 federal NDP convention. He recalls that the slogan on the button he prepared for supporters of the statement at that convention ("only the beginning") is appropriate for this book which carries on the debate raised by the statement.

Peter Warrian is presently a labour economist and consultant working in Toronto. He was formerly chair of the federal NDP Policy Review Committee and chaired the committee which in 1983 drafted the statement, *Policy and Objectives*, the "official manifesto" to which the *June 22nd Statement* was a response. From 1974 to 1983 he was on the staff of the United Steelworkers, serving as Legislative Director and later as Research Director. From 1983 to 1985 he was Executive Assistant to the President of the Ontario Public Service Employees Union. He has been a member of the Economic Policy, Pension and Energy Policy Committees of the CLC. In another age, from 1968-69, he was president of the Canadian Union of Students. He describes himself politically as an "unreconstructed 1960s person". He has published widely in the fields of labour economics, labour history and labour law. He is currently writing a book on the "postwar deal" in Canada.

June 22nd
Statement of Principles

Regina, June 30 — July 3, 1983

In the summer of 1933 delegates assembled in Regina for the first national Convention of the Co-operative Commonwealth Federation, the predecessor of the NDP. The ravages of the Great Depression had brought them together to form one party, with a determination to realize the "co-operative commonwealth", and prepared to compromise their self-interest to forge a common agenda of reform: the *Regina Manifesto*.

Among these Canadians was an optimistic and defiant insistence that ordinary people—despite major divisions of region, ethnic origin and social class—could act together, democratically and independently of powerful "vested interests", to realize the common good.

Much has changed in Canada since the *Regina Manifesto*. Stronger provincial and local governments, capable of realizing important tasks of economic and social development, have emerged. The public domain has been husbanded and, on a scale unimaginable in the 1930s, the resource sector has created new jobs and revenue for governments.

Also, since that time, Quebec has emerged as a vibrant dynamic society intent on asserting its distinct identity. Whereas the interests and ideas of men dominated society then, women now rightly demand equality.

Much, however, remains to be done. Poverty, mass unemployment, and an unacceptable concentration of power and wealth persist as moral affronts to a society which values economic and social justice.

The environment has been damaged, and the wastage will continue if not checked by strong measures. Many Canadians, having migrated in the millions from farm to city, now find themselves without a sense of community, living in large, impersonal cities and working in alienating surroundings.

Finally, the technology of war has made ours the first generation which must confront the prospect of the annihilation of our species in a nuclear holocaust.

Now, fifty years later, we need to renew that Convention's sense of urgency, of commitment to fundamental change, and of willingness to act beyond narrow self-interest.

* * *

In 1933 the Canadians who met in Regina wanted immediate and radical action to end the Depression. Delegates were critical of the federal principle as a legalistic constraint on the ability of a strong centralized government to realize the general will. Those in attendance did not foresee the advantages in decentralization of important political jurisdictions to the provinces which thereby increased the responsiveness of government to people, and permitted political change to begin in one region and spread. We can draw a measure of satisfaction from the many social changes CCF and NDP provincial governments have introduced.

In 1983 much still remains unsettled as to the nature of Canada. However the only basis for change in the Canadian federation can be respect for its regionalism, and for its duality.

We view the demand by Canadians to decentralize, where feasible, political authority as proof that Canadians want to participate more directly in the political decisions that affect their lives.

The desire to decentralize means more than provincial rights. Our cities must assume the imprint of their citizens. Credit unions and co-operatives can provide democratic alternatives to large financial and corporate institutions.

Canadians, however, also want a strong central government, strong enough to guarantee our national independence and our ability to forge a strong Canadian economy in the face of world competition. We want a Federal government which will guarantee to each of us a share of our national prosperity regardless of the region in which we live.

The unique and enduring identity of the French Canadian people is a fundamental reality of Canada. Because few French Canadians attended the 1933 Convention of our party, the delegates were to underestimate the importance Quebecois attached, and would continue to attach, to the rights of their National Assembly as the guardian of francophone culture, and as an instrument for the economic development of the only province in which French Canadians form a majority.

While we in the NDP assert the right of the Quebecois to determine freely their own future, we hope that, in the exercise of their democratic right, they do not choose sovereignty. We firmly believe that the aspirations of Quebecois are realizable within a new union which leaves important jurisdictions to a central government.

Whatever our differences may have been, it is long past due that we, in the NDP, join with those on the left in Quebec and French Canadians elsewhere, for the challenges which face us and the bonds which bind us are much greater than the differences, however profound, that have kept us apart.

* * *

The delegates in Regina in 1933 met as the clouds of war were beginning to blacken the skies of Europe and Asia. The darkness of their time pales in comparison to the endless night of nuclear holocaust which threatens this earth in 1983. Militarism is again rampant, and the merchants of death profit.

Let us on the left be clear in our condemnation of Soviet expansion and nuclear build-up. We must accept our responsibility to participate—within the context of an independent Canadian foreign policy—in the collective defence of those liberties and freedoms people have fought for centuries, first, to acquire and, then, to retain.

That said, we must with equal conviction condemn the present American Administration for its military adventurism against movements of national liberation, for its role in escalating the nuclear arms race, and for its unqualified support of the ambitions and appetites of the multinationals.

* * *

Now, as in the 1930s, the western industrial economies have suffered a serious economic crisis, and again the Right has argued that government intervention to improve economic performance would only make matters worse. To control inflation governments in the recent past, in Ottawa and other capitals, have pursued monetarist policies of restrictive credit and public spending. The result has been an immoral exchange: relative price stability at the cost of massive unemployment, particularly among the unskilled, the young, and the unprotected.

We, in the NDP, restate our commitment that government must intervene aggressively to stimulate employment during difficult economic times.

But government must also control inflation. At times, excess demand has been the cause, but in a society where powerful interests can set their prices, profits and incomes in terms of self-defined "fair shares", any economic shock that lower the real income of some launches a dynamic of price-wage spiralling to "catch up". The only available alternative to monetarism is income planning in key sectors. An incomes policy must be equitable: not a means to increase corporate profits at the expense of working people.

An incomes policy must figure as part of a larger agreement to create a new social contract in Canada. Such an agreement requires co-operation among government, labour and business. Among its major components must be a renewed commitment to full employment; government encouragement for workers to organize collectively, and to participate as equals in the management of the work place and the evaluation of new technology; better public accountability of government agencies and of Crown corporations; and development of new high-productivity sectors.

* * *

In 1983, meeting again in convention in Regina, we rededicate ourselves to the struggle for a humane and democratic society.

We affirm our belief in the worth and integrity of the human person. We oppose all efforts to denigrate, exploit or destroy that worth.

We affirm our belief in the human spirit, and in the need for political, religious and artistic freedom to permit its full expression. Cultural independence is paramount, as is the strengthening of our vital cultural institutions.

We affirm that Canada is made up of a rich diversity of peoples, a resource to be treasured.

We affirm our belief in the equality of persons, and believe each has the right to receive respect and to participate fully in our society. In particular, our aim is a society wherein men and women share responsibilities equally.

We affirm our commitment to the preservation of the family farm, other family enterprises and small business.

We affirm our belief that aboriginal peoples have the right to shape their own future out of their own past, and to possess the institutions necessary to survive and flourish.

We affirm our belief in the need for ecological priorities to guide technological and economic decisions so that valuable common resources are not depleted or polluted, and global justice becomes possible.

We affirm our belief that we, as individuals and as a nation, must do all within our power to arrest the madness of the nuclear arms race. A first step would be to declare Canada a nuclear weapons free zone.

We affirm our belief that each of us has the right to participate fully in the decisions that affect our lives, both in government and at our place of work, either through elected representatives or by direct personal participation.

We affirm our belief in the right of each person to work. We believe that each person has the right to realize his or her dignity and the fullness of his or her potential through creative and meaningful work.

We affirm our belief that government has a meaningful role to play in betterment of the human condition. We shall vigorously oppose those who exploit the public domain for private profit, thereby discrediting the principle of government intervention. We recognize that it falls to us to rescue the principle of collective action through government from those of our opponents who have debased and perverted it in the pursuit of self-aggrandizement.

We affirm our belief in the right of equal access by all Canadians to quality health, education and social services, unconstrained by the ability to pay.

We affirm our solidarity with those who are struggling everywhere for economic, political and social justice. Their struggle is our struggle. We believe in a new, just and sustainable international economic order, in which co-operation and negotiation replace the global profit strategies of the multinationals.

We affirm our belief in the right of people to associate, into trade unions and other associations, for the realization of shared interests.

We affirm our belief that as a country we have the resources, the capital, the technology, and above all else, the aspirations and skills of working men and women, required to build an alternative economic future.

It is a difficult time: a time of danger, a time of opportunity. Those who walk alone may fall victim to fear and self-doubt. We challenge Canadians to journey together as brothers and sisters in love and fellowship, knowing no fear, sharing their dreams and hopes.

The future belongs to the human spirit, and we are of that spirit.

Authorized by the
Committee in support
of the June 22nd Statement